PAVE THE TRAIL
TO CUB SCOUT

You'll discover excitement and adventure within the pages of these important Cub Scout books! Not only will you find page after page of fun, but information as well.

Bear Book. Travel through the exciting requirements and electives that lead the Cub Scout on his way to becoming a Bear. IB3228 . . . . $2.25

Webelos Book. The excitement of Scouting continues to build as this book leads the Cub Scout to Webelos with all of the Arrow of Light requirements. IB3232 . . . . $2.25

Den Chief Handbook. What can you do to become a great den chief? This book shows you what you can do and covers the pack/troop relationship. IB3211 . . . . $2.10

Cub Scout Magic. Dazzle your audience with nearly 200 fantastic stunts, tricks and puzzles. You can become a master of magicians! IB3219 . . . . $5.75

No. 70-944

5/86

This Is My Wolf Cub Scout Book

I am _____

I live at _____

_____

_____

Den _____ Pack _____ of _____

YOU MAY BE A CUB SCOUT, IF:

**You have completed the 1st grade or
You are 8 years of age.**

Contents

Illustrations of Akela by Robert Depew

Copyright 1986
BOY SCOUTS OF AMERICA • IRVING, TEXAS
ISBN 0-8395-3234-2, No. 3234
Printed in U.S.A. 1986 Printing

Parent Guide

How to help your boy follow the Bobcat, Wolf, and Arrow Point Trails

I f you could give your boy the greatest gift of all, what would it be? It wouldn't be money or anything money can buy. Whether you are rich or poor, the greatest gift is within your power because that gift is helping a boy become a self-reliant person with a good feeling about himself and a genuine concern for others.

For more than 75 years the Boy Scouts of America has helped families share this priceless gift with boys.

Baden-Powell, the founder of Scouting, based Cub Scouting on one of the stories in Rudyard Kipling's *Jungle Books*. It was called "Mowgli's Brothers." We know it as "The Story of Akela and Mowgli." Read the story twice, once to yourself and the second time to your Cub Scout.

4   THE STORY OF AKELA AND MOWGLI

THE STORY OF AKELA AND MOWGLI

Once upon a time in the jungles of India on a warm summer evening, Father Wolf awoke, stretched his paws, and prepared to go hunting.

The moon shone into the mouth of the cave where Mother Wolf lay sleeping with their four young cubs. Suddenly, a shadow crossed the opening of the cave and a whining voice said, "Good Hunting, O' Chief of the Wolves, and good luck to your children." It was Tabaqui, the sneaky little jackal who, because he is too lazy to hunt for himself, picks up scraps left by other animals.

Father Wolf told him, "There is no food here, but come in if you wish."

Tabaqui said, "For a poor animal like myself a dry bone is a feast," and in no time at all he was cracking away on a bone at the back of the cave. Now Tabaqui was always ready to make trouble and to talk about others. He said, "Shere Khan, the mighty tiger, has changed his hunting ground. He hunts in these hills for the next moon." (Shere Khan was the tiger who lived about twenty miles away, near the big river.)

Father Wolf said, "By the Law of the Jungle, he had no right to change his hunting ground. He will scare the animals away for miles around."

Tabaqui said, "I could have saved myself the trouble of telling you. You can hear him now in the jungle below." And he trotted off to find the tiger.

Father and Mother Wolf listened. From the valley below, they could hear the angry whine of a tiger who had caught nothing and didn't care if the whole jungle knew it.

"The fool," said Father Wolf, "to start a night's hunting with all that noise!" The whine changed to a humming-purr, which is the noise a tiger makes when he is hunting man. Father Wolf said, "Are there not enough frogs and beetles that he must hunt Man?"

Just then there was a most untigerish howl from Shere Khan, and Mother Wolf said, "He missed! What happened?"

Father Wolf ran out a few paces and looked down to a clearing where there were several woodcutters' huts. He said, "Shere Khan has had no more sense than to jump at the woodcutters' fire. He burned his feet! Tabaqui is with him and they have frightened all the people away."

"Listen," Mother Wolf said, "something is coming up the hill. Get ready!"

Father Wolf crouched and sprang, but as he sprang, he stopped himself in midair because what he saw was a little baby boy!

"Man!" he said. "A man cub. Look!"

"I have never seen one," Mother Wolf said. "Bring him to me."

Father Wolf brought him into the cave and put him down beside Mother Wolf.

6   THE STORY OF AKELA AND MOWGLI

The baby snuggled close to the young wolf cubs. "How little he is," said Mother Wolf.

Suddenly, the moonlight was blocked from the door of the cave by the great head and shoulders of Shere Khan.

"What does Shere Khan want?" said Father Wolf with angry eyes.

"The man-cub!" said Shere Khan. "Give him to me!"

Father Wolf said, "The wolves take orders only from Akela, the head of the wolf pack. The man-cub is ours."

The tiger's roar filled the cave with thunder. "The man-cub is mine. Give him to me!" said Shere Khan.

Mother Wolf sprang up quickly and said, "The man-cub is ours. You have frightened his family away. He shall not be killed. He shall live to run with the pack and hunt with the pack."

Shere Khan knew he could not fight the two wolves in the cave; therefore, he went away growling, snarling, and saying, "We will see what the pack has to say about this man-cub."

When the tiger had gone, Father Wolf said, "Shere Khan is right. What will the pack say?" But Mother Wolf had decided to keep him. And they called him Mowgli ("the frog") because his skin was smooth and without hair. Mowgli stayed with the young cubs.

When they were old enough to run, Father and Mother Wolf set off with them one night, through the jungle to a meeting of the wolf pack at the Council Rock. The Law

of the Jungle states that wolves must gather to look over the new wolf cubs of the pack, so that they will know them and take care of them when they see them in the jungle.

As each young wolf was pushed into the circle, Akela, the great leader of the wolf pack, sitting high on the Council Rock, called, "Look at each cub, O' Wolves. Look well." At last it was Mowgli's turn and Mother Wolf pushed him into the circle where he sat playing with some stones in the moonlight. Akela did not even twitch an ear as he called, "Look well, O' Wolves."

From outside the circle came a roar from Shere Khan. "The man-cub is mine. Give him to me." Some of the wolves took up the cry, "What do we want with a man-cub in the pack?"

There is a law that says if there is an argument as to the right of a cub to join the pack, two people must speak for him. Akela asked, "Who speaks for this cub?"

At first there was no answer, but then Baloo, the sleepy brown bear who teaches the cubs the Law of the Pack, stepped into the circle and said, "I will speak for the man-cub. Let him join the pack and I, myself, will teach him the law and the ways of the jungle."

"We need another," said Akela. "Who beside Baloo speaks?"

An inky black shadow dripped silently into the circle. It was Bagheera, the black panther, the mighty hunter who teaches the cubs the skills of the jungle. In his soft silky voice he said, "If there is a question about the right of a cub to join the pack, his life may be bought at a price. Isn't that the law?"

'Yes," said the pack.

"Then to Baloo's good word, I will add fresh meat which is in the valley below, if you will accept Mowgli into the pack."

The wolves cried, "Let him join. What harm can a man-cub do?" They looked him over; then, one by one, the wolves went down the hill, leaving Mowgli with Father and Mother Wolf, Baloo, and Bagheera at the Council Rock with Akela. Akela said, "Now take him away and teach him the Law of the Pack."

And that is how Mowgli joined the Seeonee Wolf Pack.

THE FAMILY

While the purpose of Cub Scouting is serious, the program itself is fun because you take the part of the wise Akela and your boy takes the part of Mowgli who must learn from you how to become a resourceful Wolf Cub Scout.

You are one of many adults who work with a Cub Scout. As a parent, your responsibility is for one boy. The den leader is Akela for all the boys in the den.

Whether a boy succeeds in Cub Scouting or quits for lack of interest is up to you! From the time he makes his first promise—to do my best—until he crosses the Webelos Scout bridge to a Boy Scout troop, he needs your guidance, enthusiasm, and active participation.

To help a boy succeed in his Cub Scout activities and advancement, you don't have to be an expert in Scouting. But you do need to spend time with the boy, learn his concerns and problems, and help him solve them.

Child Abuse

Child abuse falls into many forms—physical, mental, sexual, and even verbal—and it can be difficult to spot. But as a parent you can teach your Cub Scout what to do when anyone makes him feel fearful or ashamed, or touches him in an inappropriate manner. Explain that his body belongs only to himself, and that he has the right to say "No!" Tell him to report any inappropriate activity to you immediately.

Akela's OK

As you thumb through the book, you'll see constant references to "Akela's OK." That's you! A boy can't get credit for any of his requirements until you, Akela, approve them. As you watch a boy complete requirements with your advice and help, you'll soon find that you're working together and that's one of the reasons for the Cub Scouting—families working together and having fun."

1 BOBCAT TRAIL	*Tina Brown* Akela's OK	*5-16-86* Date	*Beverly Jones* Recorded by den leader

Notes for Akela

Throughout the *Wolf Cub Scout Book*, special notes for you are printed along with the requirements for special projects which require the supervision and participation of adults. Watch for these "Notes for Akela." They are printed in a smaller type size for your easy identification.

The Bobcat Trail

In Rudyard Kipling's story the black panther, Bagheera, is the mighty hunter who teaches the cubs the skills of the jungle. In Cub Scouting we use the symbol of the Bobcat. You'll find his trail on pages 20 through 29. Along this trail are the Cub Scout Promise, the Law of the Pack, and the Cub Scout motto. These are the three most important things a boy must learn because they will help him through all of the trails of Scouting.

Bobcat badge

When you and your boy have followed the seven tracks of the Bobcat, your boy may wear his Bobcat badge. It will be presented at the pack meeting.

The Den and the Pack

Cub Scouting is for the whole family and neighborhoods of families. Turn to pages 30 through 37. There you will read about the den and pack and how you and your boy fit in.

As a member of a Cub Scout den, a boy meets with his den leaders and fellow Cub Scouts in the home of a parent. In den meetings, the Cub Scouts work on projects, learn games, songs, and tricks to be presented at a monthly pack meeting.

You may be asked to help at den meetings, but your main obligation is to attend the monthly pack meetings to see your boy's den and others in action. At the pack meeting held in the meeting place of the organization that operates the pack, you and the boys will take part in a lively program of activities based on a theme of the month.

If possible, the whole family should attend and enjoy the fun and watch the Cub Scouts receive their awards.

The Wolf Trail

The next adventure is the Wolf Trail from page 38 through page 103. This is a big adventure for a boy, one the Boy Scouts of America hopes all boys will complete. The Bobcat trail has only seven tracks; the Wolf trail is much longer than the Bobcat's.

When you have okayed the tracks your boy has filled in for all 12 achievements, he may become a Wolf Cub Scout. How quickly your boy progresses is up to him and you. He should do his best to complete each track, that's a part of the promise he made to become a Bobcat and it is the Cub Scout motto—Do Your Best. Don't okay a track if you both know that he can do a better job. Go on to something else, then come back to the problem track.

The important thing is to keep him interested.

PROGRESS TOWARD RANKS ON THE WOLF TRAIL. Your boy doesn't have to wait until he completes his entire Wolf trail before being recognized for his work. When he completes any three achievements, his den leader can present the Progress Toward Ranks patch to him. It's a diamond with a leather thong and a gold bead attached. Each time he completes three achievements he will receive another gold bead. After he gets his fourth gold bead, he will receive his Wolf badge at a pack meeting.

As your boy completes the requirements for the achievements on the Wolf trail, be sure to review his work and sign his book in the place for *Akela's OK*. At his next den meeting, he should show his book to his den leader who will record his progress and sign the book on the line provided.

1 *Tina Brown* 5-16-86   *Beverly Jones*
WOLF TRAIL   Akela's OK   Date   Recorded by den leader

The Arrow Point Trail

If your Wolf Cub Scout has not completed second grade (or reached his ninth birthday), he can search the Arrow Point trail. On the Wolf trail, the main sections were called achievements, things that we would like all boys to do. On the Arrow Point trail, the main sections are called electives, choices that a boy can make on his own and with your guidance.

THE FAMILY

To earn a Gold Arrow Point to wear beneath his Wolf badge, the boy must complete any 10 elective projects of the more than 100 choices shown in the book. If he does 10 more, he qualifies for a Silver Arrow Point to wear beneath the Gold. These are presented at the pack meeting after he receives his Wolf badge.

1 | *Tina Brown*   5-16-86   *Beverly Jones*
ARROW POINT TRAIL   Akela's OK   Date   Recorded by den leader

Badges Point the Way

Offering badges is a way to provide recognition and to encourage participation. The Bobcat, Wolf, Gold, and Silver Arrow Point badges are material rewards that mean a great deal to boys who work to earn them. In doing these different things, the Boy Scouts of America expects boys to grow in a number of ways.

Remember that the plan is flexible and can be adapted to suit your needs and situation. It is not necessary to buy special equipment; however, it is necessary is to be imaginative and to make do with what you have.

Do Your Best as Akela

The Boy Scouts of America hereby authorizes you who have read this Parent Guide to act as Akela and to indicate your willingness to serve by signing below.

I/We will be Akela in this *Wolf Cub Scout Book*:

Signature _____ Date _____

Signature _____ Date _____

Signature _____ Date _____

SPORTS AND PHYSICAL FITNESS

The Cub Scout sports and physical fitness program provides every Cub Scout an opportunity to become acquainted with, and to participate in, all kinds of sports. The program includes summer and winter sports, both indoors and outdoors, team, active, and less-active types. When done correctly, the program is an active physical fitness program for Cub Scouts.

A Cub Scout may participate in a sports program in his unit, in his community, or by himself. Cub Scout sports emphasizes participation of the family by involving an adult teammate. There is recognition for both participation and good performance by the Cub Scout and his adult teammate. Throughout, the Cub Scout is encouraged to learn and to practice good sportsmanship and to "do his best."

Each pamphlet provides the basics for the beginner and describes how you can participate.

Additional pamphlets are available for your Cub Scout and his adult teammate. These pamphlets were developed in cooperation with experts and national associations.

Three points of sportsmanship are stressed continually in the program of the Boy Scouts of America. These will provide many opportunities for adult/Cub Scout discussions.

Honesty is a key to success. It is the foundation for everything we do. Without it our society could not exist. The freedom we all cherish is based on honest relationships. Our day-to-day activities are based on the promises of people to people.

Just as important is young people's trust in their parents. Honesty on the part of both helps build that trust. It also contributes to our children's well-being and confidence as they meet new people and face life's problems.

Fair play is involved in belonging to more than just a family. It relates to the Cub Scout den, neighborhood, and even the country. Everyone has a share in whatever is at stake.

Respect for others should happen regardless of age or position. Maintaining respect for a person is important, even if we dislike that person's actions. Respect for others starts in the home and works its way outward. Courteous behavior opens doors to opportunities that otherwise might remain closed.

It must be remembered, however, that discussions you have with youth may be meaningless if your own example of behavior is inconsistent with what you say. Remember, "your actions speak louder than your words."

AKELA IS YOUR
FRIEND

You have heard how Mowgli met Akela. Just as that story said, in a real wolf pack all the wolves look to Akela, the leader, for guidance—when to work, when to learn, when to play.

Akela makes sure each young wolf in the pack gets the chance to learn about the world, and how to get along with other members of the pack.

There are times when Akela romps and plays games with members of the pack. But there are times when Akela, with a movement of his head or a steady gaze, commands the young wolves' attention.

Akela, the wolf pack leader, is caring and wise. He is both a friend and a teacher.

Like your parents, your teachers, and other adults who help you learn, Akela is your guide.

Throughout the pages of this book, Akela will guide you to your place in the pack. Along the Wolf trail, you will learn the Cub Scout Promise and the Law of the Pack.

You will learn new skills. You will try new things. And Akela, your guide, will help you begin your exciting trail through Cub Scouting, and onward to Boy Scouting.

COME! BE A PART OF THE PACK. FOLLOW THE TRAIL.

WE BEGIN OUR TRAIL BY FOLLOWING AKELA'S FRIEND, THE BOBCAT. FOLLOW HIS TRAIL FIRST TO BECOME A BOBCAT CUB SCOUT, AND TO EARN YOUR PLACE IN THE PACK.

Bobcat Trail

WELCOME TO OUR PACK!

Say Hi to my friend the Bobcat. He has seven things for you to do.

HE
SAYS

Follow
my
**BOBCAT
TRAIL**

**Fill in this track
when you have done it.**

Learn and say the Cub Scout Promise.

I, ..., promise to do my best
(your name)
To do my duty to God and my country,
To help other people, and
To obey the Law of the Pack.

Duty to God means
Put God first. Do what you
know God wants you to do.

And my country means
Do what you can for your
country. Be proud that you
are an American.

**To help other people
means**
Do things for others that
would please them.

**Obey the Law of the Pack
means**
Be a good Cub Scout. Be
proud that you are one.

**When you say
you will do
something,
that is a
promise.**

**When you can say the Promise,
fill in my track.**

_____   _____   _____
Akela's OK   Date   Recorded by den leader

BOBCAT TRAIL   21

Say the Law of the Pack.
Tell what it means.

The Law of the Pack

The Cub Scout follows Akela.
The Cub Scout helps the pack go.
The pack helps the Cub Scout grow.
The Cub Scout gives goodwill.

The Cub Scout follows Akela (say Ah-KAY-la).

Akela is a good leader.
Your mother or father is Akela.
In the pack, your Cubmaster is Akela.
Your den leader is Akela.
At school, your teacher is Akela.

The Cub Scout helps the pack go.

Come to all the meetings. Do what you can to help.
Think of others in the pack.

The pack helps the Cub Scout grow.

You can have fun when you are a part of the pack.
Learn things from others. Do things with them.

The Cub Scout gives goodwill.

Smile. Be happy. Do things that make others happy.
They don't have to be big things. Little things help,
too.

**When you can say the Law
of the Pack and tell what
it means, fill in my track.**

Akela's OK	Date	Recorded by den leader

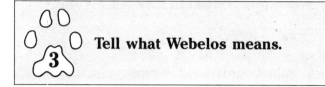

Tell what Webelos means.

Webelos is a Cub Scout secret.
Cub Scouts know the secret. It is—
  We'll Be Loyal Scouts

We'll
Be
Loyal
Scouts } **WeBeLoS**

Being loyal means that you will keep
the Cub Scout Promise.

The Webelos Arrow
of Light is another
secret. It points the
right way to go every
day of the week.

**When you know what Webelos
means, fill in my track.**

_____   _____ _____
Akela's OK   Date   Recorded by den leader

**Show the Cub Scout sign.
Tell what it means.**

**Make the sign with
your right hand and
with your arm held
straight up.**

The two fingers stand for two
parts of the Promise—"to help
other people" and "to obey."
They look like a wolf's ears
ready to listen to Akela.

Give the Cub Scout sign when
you say the Cub Scout Promise
or the Law of the Pack.

**When you can give the sign and tell
what it means, fill in the track.**

Akela's OK   Date   Recorded by den leader

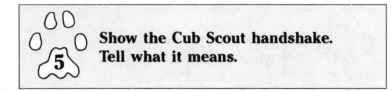

**Show the Cub Scout handshake.
Tell what it means.**

Here's how to shake hands with another Cub Scout. Hold out your right hand just as you always do to shake hands. Put your first two fingers along the inside of the other boy's wrist.

This means that you help and that you obey the Law of the Pack.

**When you can shake hands
as a Cub Scout, fill in my track.**

Akela's OK   Date   Recorded by den leader

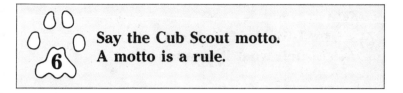

**Say the Cub Scout motto.
A motto is a rule.**

**DO YOUR BEST is
the Cub Scout motto.**

It means—

When you play a game, do your best to help your team win.

When you study in school, do your best to learn from your teacher.

When you help at home, do your best to help your family. Whatever you do, do your best.

**When you know the motto
and can tell what it means,
fill in my track.**

Akela's OK   Date   Recorded by den leader

**Give the Cub Scout salute.
Tell what it means.**

Salute with your right hand. Hold your fingers as you do for the Cub Scout sign. Keep the two straight fingers close together. Touch the tips of those fingers to your cap. If you are not wearing a cap, touch your eyebrow.

A salute is a way to show respect to your leaders. It shows that you look up to them and respect them. We salute the flag to show respect to our country.

**When you can give the Cub Scout
salute and tell what it means,
fill in my track.**

Akela's OK   Date   Recorded by den leader

If you have filled in seven of my tracks, you are my friend.

Now you are a Bobcat Cub Scout and you can wear my badge.

YOUR DEN

Your den is a group of boys who live in your general neighborhood. You may know and play with most of them.

About once a week you will meet with your den. Your den leader, the adult in charge of the meetings, will be Akela.

Your den leader will help guide you through the exciting Wolf trail that is part of the Cub Scout adventure. You will have fun doing that and other things.

You and other boys in your den will have fun getting ready for the pack meeting in many of your den meetings.

Cub Scouting is fun, and much of that fun starts in your den.

The den meeting is usually held in somebody's home. It may be held in your home.

What do you do at a den meeting? Lots of things. You'd better be on time or you will miss something.

When you get there, Cub Scouts may be playing a game or doing a puzzle.

When all the Cub Scouts are there, it is time to start the meeting.

You may salute the flag or say the Cub Scout Promise.

Maybe you will play a game that has something to do with the month's show idea; we call it a theme. Or you could do a stunt or skit or make something.

Before the meeting ends, you may be a part of the living circle ceremony. Hold out your left hand—palm down, and thumb out. Hold the thumb of the boy on your left.

DO	SAY
Raise the living circle	AH
Lower it	KAY
Raise it	LA
Lower it	WE'LL
Raise it	DO
Lower it	OUR
Raise it	BEST

Or you may end the meeting with this Cub Scout prayer in Indian sign language.

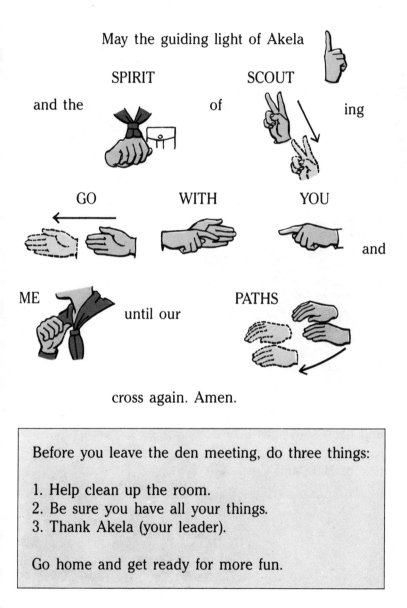

May the guiding light of Akela

and the SPIRIT of SCOUT ing

GO WITH YOU and

ME until our PATHS

cross again. Amen.

Before you leave the den meeting, do three things:

1. Help clean up the room.
2. Be sure you have all your things.
3. Thank Akela (your leader).

Go home and get ready for more fun.

YOUR PACK

Wolves from many dens run in packs. The pack is one big happy family.

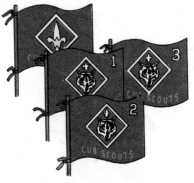

Your den belongs to a pack. You will meet members of other dens at a pack meeting.

A pack meeting is a show and each show has a new idea, such as Cub Scout Fair or Blue and Gold.

Each den takes a part in the show. But pack meetings are not just for Cub Scouts. Pack meetings are for families. They watch while you and other Cub Scouts do your stuff and get your badges.

Your pack may belong to a church or a school or something like that. Your pack meets there.

The pack leader is called a Cubmaster. The Cubmaster is Akela for the pack.

YOUR UNIFORM

The Blue and Gold

The blue in your uniform is for truth. Gold is for sunlight, good cheer, and happiness. When you wear the Cub Scout uniform, people will know you are trying to be good and helpful.

Earn It

Uniforms cost money. You can help pay for yours. There are jobs that you can do at home or near where you live. Tell your folks you want to help. Everybody should have a job to do and you should want to do your share.

Buy It

You cannot buy your uniform in just any store. Ask your leader where to buy it. Only Cub Scouts can buy a Cub Scout uniform. You must show your membership card.

Wear It

Wear your uniform to den and pack meetings. Wear it whenever you take part in something Cub Scouts do. Keep your uniform clean and neat. Hang it in a closet or fold it and put it in a drawer or on a shelf.

Now, follow my

My track is different
from the Bobcat's. Cats
don't show their claws,
but wolves and dogs do.

Wolf

Bobcat

**Fill in my tracks as you follow
my trail. Not all the tracks have
to be filled in. Sometimes you
can choose.**

49 TRACKS OF ACHIEVEMENT

1. Feats of Skill
   ◄— Do one —►
   | a | b | c | d | e | f | g | h | i | j | k |

2. Your Flag
   | a | b | c | d | e |

3. Keep Your
   Body Healthy
   | a | b | c |

4. Know Your Home
   and Community
   | a | b | c | d | e |

5. Tools for Fixing
   and Building
   | a | b | c | d | e |

6. Start a
   Collection
   | a | b |

7. Your Living World
   | a | b | c | d | e |

8. Cooking and Eating
   | a | b | c | d | e |

9. Be Safe at Home
   and on the Street
   | a | b | c | d |

10. Family Fun
    ◄— Do two —►
    | a | b | c | d | e |

11. Duty to God
    | a | b | c |

12. Making Choices
    ◄— Do four —►
    | a | b | c | d | e | f | g | h | i |

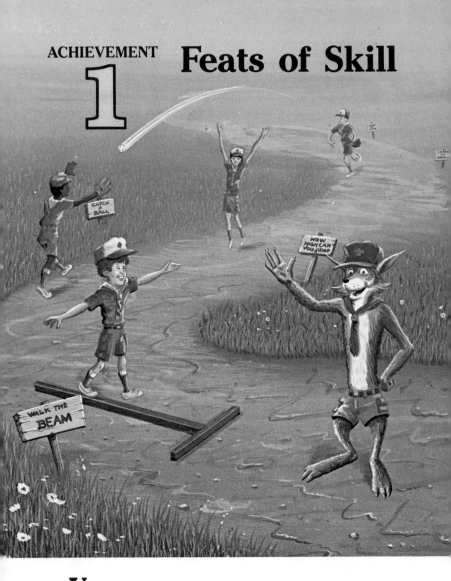

ACHIEVEMENT 1   Feats of Skill

You are growing. You are getting stronger. Try these feats of skill. Test your speed. Test your balance. Test your strength.

REQUIREMENTS

1a. Play catch with someone 10 steps away. Play until you can throw and catch.

| a | Akela's OK | Date | Recorded by den leader |

1b. Walk a line back and forth. Do it sideways, too. Then walk the edge of a board six steps each way.

NOTE for Akela: If a physician certifies that a Cub Scout's physical condition for an indeterminable time won't permit him to do three of these requirements, the Cubmaster and pack committee may authorize substitution of any three arrow point electives.

| b | Akela's OK | Date | Recorded by den leader |

FEATS OF SKILL

1c. Do a front roll.

c Akela's OK   Date   Recorded by den leader

1d. Do a back roll.

WOLF TRAIL

d Akela's OK   Date   Recorded by den leader

1e. Do a falling forward roll.

e Akela's OK   Date   Recorded by den leader

DO THIS ➡

1f. **See how high you can jump.**

Count down from 10 to 0 and coil your body for a blast-off.

When you come to 0, yell blast-off and jump as high into the air as you can. Land on your feet.

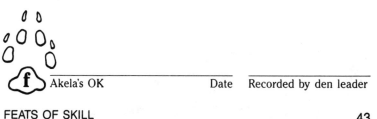

f Akela's OK   Date   Recorded by den leader

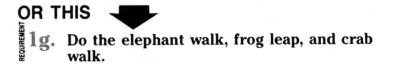

OR THIS

REQUIREMENT 1g. Do the elephant walk, frog leap, and crab walk.

Elephant walk

Frog leap

Crab walk

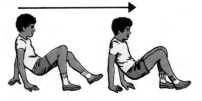

Akela's OK _____ Date _____ Recorded by den leader

**g**

WOLF TRAIL

OR THIS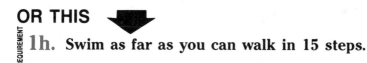

1h. Swim as far as you can walk in 15 steps.

Hold onto something and move through the water the same distance, just by kicking your feet.

Do both of these in shallow water with a grown-up who swims well.

NOTE for Akela: Measure at the side of the pool, or along the shore of a pond or lake.

h Akela's OK   Date   Recorded by den leader

OR THIS

1i. Using a basketball or playground ball—

Bounce pass

Baseball pass

Do a chest pass.

Akela's OK   Date   Recorded by den leader

OR THIS

REQUIREMENT 1j. Do a frog stand.

(j) Akela's OK _____ Date _____ Recorded by den leader

OR THIS

REQUIREMENT 1k. Run or jog for 10 minutes.

Or jog in place for 10 minutes.

(k) Akela's OK _____ Date _____ Recorded by den leader

ACHIEVEMENT 2

Your Flag

Your flag stands for our country. Learn some ways to honor your flag.

2a. Give the Pledge of Allegiance to the flag of the United States of America. Tell what it means.

I pledge allegiance
to the flag of the
United States of America
and to the Republic
for which it stands,
one Nation under God,
indivisible, with liberty
and justice for all.

A **pledge** is a promise.
Allegiance is to be true.
Republic is our kind of government.
Nation is a country.
God is the one we worship.
Indivisible is one that cannot be
divided into pieces or parts.
Liberty is freedom for you and for others.
Justice is what is right and fair.

(a) Akela's OK   Date   Recorded by den leader

2b. Lead a flag ceremony in your den. Here are some ideas:

Get your den to stand in a straight line and face the flag. Salute and say the Pledge of Allegiance.

Flag
X

OR

Stand in a square formation. Bring in the flag. Salute and say the Cub Scout Promise.

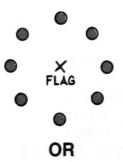

X
FLAG

OR

Stand in a circle around the flag. Salute and give the Pledge of Allegiance.

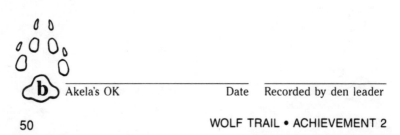

b Akela's OK

Date   Recorded by den leader

2c. Tell how to respect and take care of the flag. Show three ways to display the flag.

Be careful not to—

> 1. LET THE FLAG GET DIRTY.

> 2. LET THE FLAG GET TORN.

> 3. LET THE FLAG TOUCH THE GROUND.

Can you think of other ways
to care for your flag?

Display the
flag inside

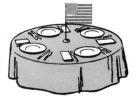

and
outside

from your windows.

_____ _____ _____
Akela's OK   Date   Recorded by den leader

YOUR FLAG   51

2d. Learn about your state flag.

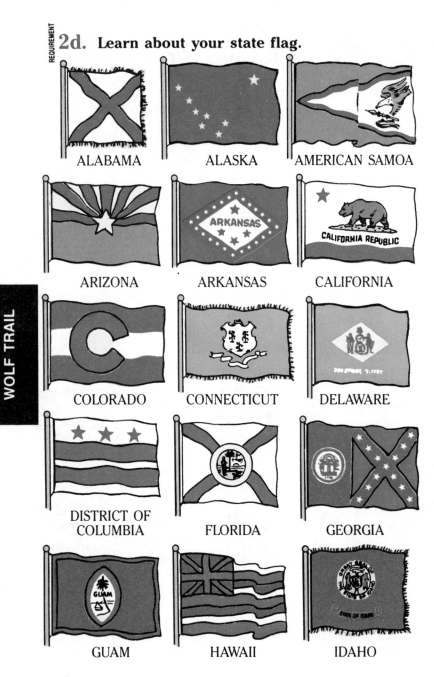

ALABAMA ALASKA AMERICAN SAMOA

ARIZONA ARKANSAS CALIFORNIA

COLORADO CONNECTICUT DELAWARE

DISTRICT OF COLUMBIA FLORIDA GEORGIA

GUAM HAWAII IDAHO

WOLF TRAIL

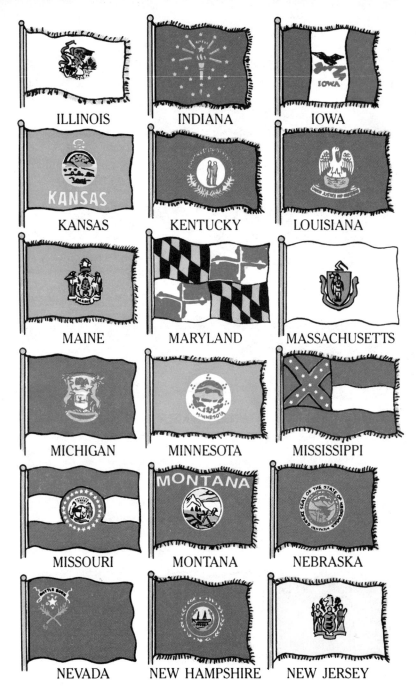

ILLINOIS INDIANA IOWA

KANSAS KENTUCKY LOUISIANA

MAINE MARYLAND MASSACHUSETTS

MICHIGAN MINNESOTA MISSISSIPPI

MISSOURI MONTANA NEBRASKA

NEVADA NEW HAMPSHIRE NEW JERSEY

NEW MEXICO   NEW YORK   NORTH CAROLINA

NORTH DAKOTA   OHIO   OKLAHOMA

OREGON   PENNSYLVANIA   PUERTO RICO

RHODE ISLAND   SOUTH CAROLINA   SOUTH DAKOTA

TENNESSEE   TEXAS   UTAH

VERMONT   VIRGIN ISLANDS   VIRGINIA

WASHINGTON   WEST VIRGINIA   WISCONSIN

WYOMING

2d. **Learn how to display your state flag.**

State flag with U.S. flag and pack flag

 Akela's OK   Date   Recorded by den leader

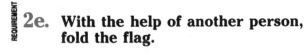

2e. **With the help of another person, fold the flag.**

WOLF TRAIL

Salute as the flag is being lowered. After it is down, fold it and put it in a safe place.

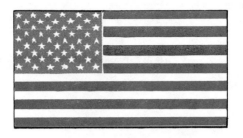

Fold to this.

Then fold again.

Fold corner up, over, and down until it looks like this.

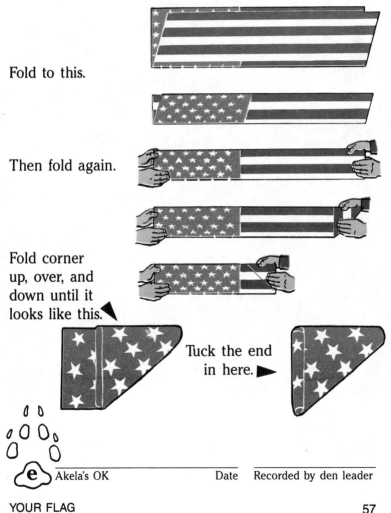

Tuck the end in here. ▶

Akela's OK   Date   Recorded by den leader

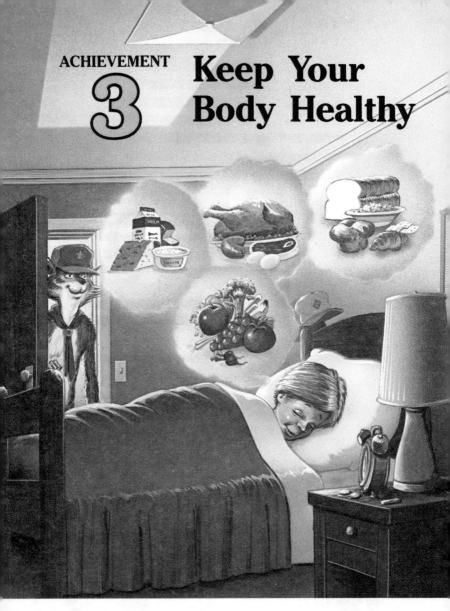

ACHIEVEMENT 3

Keep Your Body Healthy

Be healthy and strong. Learn what to do to be healthy. Keep active to be strong.

3a. Show that you know and follow the seven rules of health.

1. Take baths or showers often. Use soap.
2. Wash your hands before meals and after using the toilet.
3. Brush your teeth before you go to bed and after breakfast. Brush your teeth or rinse your mouth after eating.
4. Drink lots of water.
5. Eat different kinds of food. Do most of your eating at mealtime. Stay away from too many sweets.
6. Run and play outdoors.
7. Get the sleep you need.

(a) Akela's OK _____ Date ___ Recorded by den leader

3b. Tell three ways to stop the spread of colds.

1. If you have a cold, stay away from other people.

2. Get lots of rest.

3. Turn your head away from others when you sneeze or cough. Cover your mouth and nose.

b Akela's OK   Date   Recorded by den leader

3c. Show what to do for a small cut.

1. Tell a grown-up about the cut.

3. Wash it with soap and water, and then dry it.

2. Let the cut bleed a little.

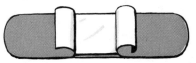

4. Cover it with a stick-on bandage. For a big cut, get help fast.

Akela's OK   Date   Recorded by den leader

KEEP YOUR BODY HEALTHY   61

ACHIEVEMENT 4

Know Your Home and Communit

Sometimes you must be home alone. If you can take care of yourself, no one will worry. You will be safe and happy. Here are some things to do.

4a. Write down the phone numbers you need to have. Put them by your phone.

Police _____

Fire _____

Doctor _____

Mother at work _____

Father at work _____

Family friend _____

a Akela's OK _____ Date _____ Recorded by den leader

REQUIREMENT

4b. If someone comes to the door and wants to come in—

I will _____

_____

_____

_____

_____

NOTE for Akela: Discuss with your boy what to do if someone wants to come in when your boy is home alone.

b Akela's OK _____ Date _____ Recorded by den leader

4c. If someone calls on the phone—

I will _____

_____

_____

_____

NOTE for Akela: Discuss with your boy
what to say if someone calls and your
boy is home alone.

c Akela's OK   Date   Recorded by den leader

4d. When I leave our home I will—

_____ Turn off lights

_____ Close and lock windows

_____ Turn off water

_____ Take care of pet

_____ Have my key

_____ Lock all doors

NOTE for Akela: Help your boy to make sure everything is taken care of before
he leaves the house.

d Akela's OK   Date   Recorded by den leader

4e. Talk with others in your home about helping. Agree on the home jobs you will do.

JOB	WHEN	DONE			

NOTE for Akela: You can teach your boy responsibility by helping him find jobs he can do to help you around the home.

Akela's OK   Date   Recorded by den leader

KNOW YOUR HOME AND COMMUNITY   65

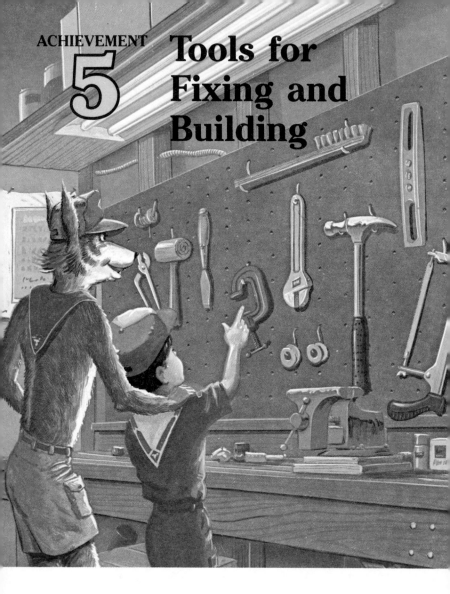

ACHIEVEMENT 5

Tools for Fixing and Building

You can make something, if you know how to use tools. You can fix things that are broken.

66   WOLF TRAIL • ACHIEVEMENT 5

Point out and name eight tools. Do this at home, or go to a hardware store with a grown-up. Tell what each tool does.

Plane to smooth wood

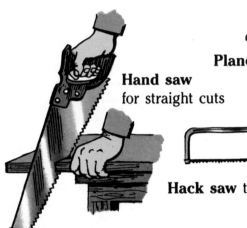

Hand saw for straight cuts

Hack saw to cut metal

File to smooth metal

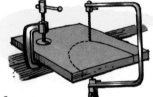

C-clamp to hold things in place

Coping saw for cutting curves

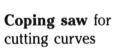

Claw hammer to drive nails and and pull them out

Plunger to open clogged drains

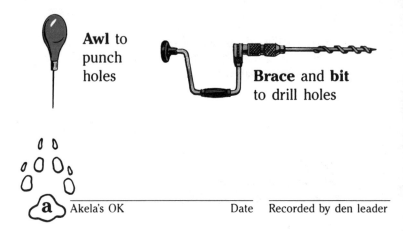

Awl to punch holes

Brace and **bit** to drill holes

5b. Show how to use pliers.

Slip-joint pliers

Slip the joint this way for small jobs.

Slip the joint this way for big jobs.

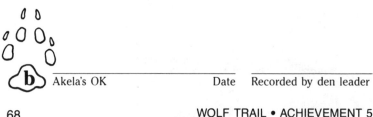

1. Start a hole in the wood with an awl or a nail.

2. A screw with soap on it is easier to turn.

3. Twist the screw into the hole.

4.

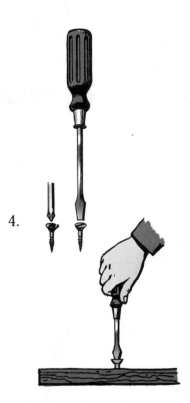

5. Turn the screw until the head is in the wood.

Akela's OK   Date   Recorded by den leader

REQUIREMENT **5d.** **Show how to use a hammer.**

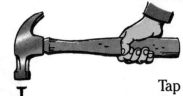

Tap a nail to
get it started.

Lift up the hammer
and drop it on
the nail. Let
the hammer
do the work.

Push

**Block of
wood**

If you bend the nail,
pull it out this way.

Akela's OK   Date   Recorded by den leader

5e. Use a pattern or a plan to make a birdhouse, a set of bookends, or something else useful.

 Akela's OK   Date   Recorded by den leader

You can collect almost anything. Put the things together so that you can show them to your family, den, and pack.

6a. Make a collection of anything you like. Start with 10 things. Put them together in a neat way.

Use an empty egg carton for stones or things like that.

Hold shells in place with wire or glue.

If you collect insects, pin them to cardboard. Wrap your display with plastic.

Use stamp hinges to
put stamps in a book.

Paste the stamp hinge
to the back of the stamp.
Then fold it down.

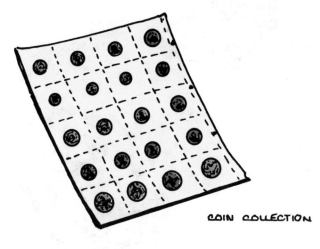

COIN COLLECTION

LEAF COLLECTION

PATCH COLLECTION

a Akela's OK   Date   Recorded by den leader

REQUIREMENT

6b. Show and explain your collection to another person.

I showed and explained my collection to _____

_____

_____

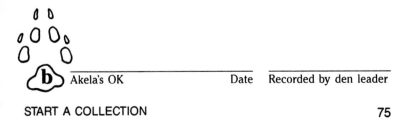

b Akela's OK   Date   Recorded by den leader

START A COLLECTION

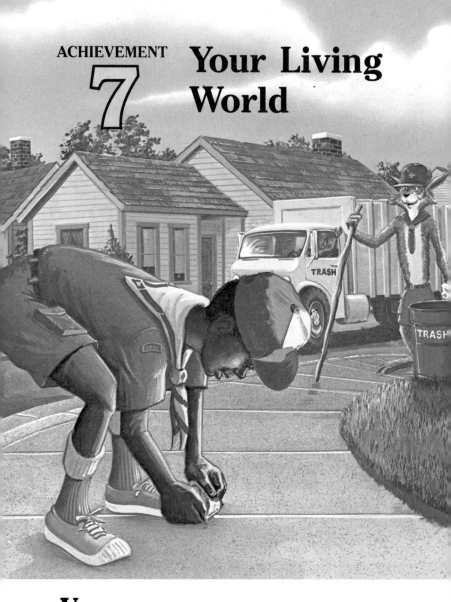

ACHIEVEMENT 7

Your Living World

Your world is the only one you have. Take care of it. Find out how to make it better. Learn how it can help you.

76   WOLF TRAIL • ACHIEVEMENT 7

7a. **Pick up litter you see. Put it where it belongs. Or recycle it.**

Aluminum cans

a Akela's OK   Date   Recorded by den leader

7b. **List 10 ways your neighborhood gets dirty. Don't forget the air and water.**

1. _____
2. _____
3. _____
4. _____
5. _____
6. _____
7. _____
8. _____
9. _____
10. _____

b Akela's OK   Date   Recorded by den leader

REQUIREMENT **7c. Write three ways to make where you live more beautiful. Then do them.**

1. ______________________________

____

2. ______________________________

____

3. ______________________________

____

c ______________________ ______________________

Akela's OK Date Recorded by den leader

WOLF TRAIL

REQUIREMENT **7d. Cut out three or four stories from newspapers or magazines that tell how people are protecting our living world.**

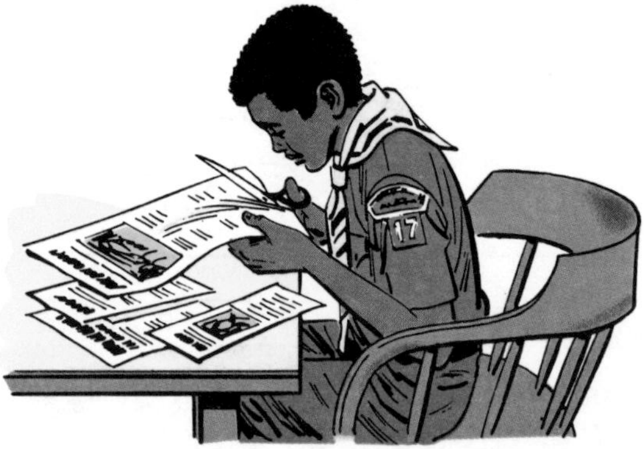

d ______________________ ______________________

Akela's OK Date Recorded by den leader

7e. **Energy is a resource. List three ways you can save energy. Save energy by doing them.**

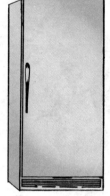

Turn the lights off.

Keep the refrigerator door closed.

1. _____
   _____
2. _____
   _____
3. _____
   _____

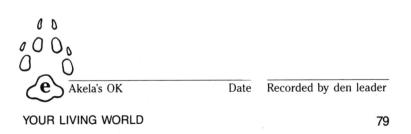

Akela's OK   Date   Recorded by den leader

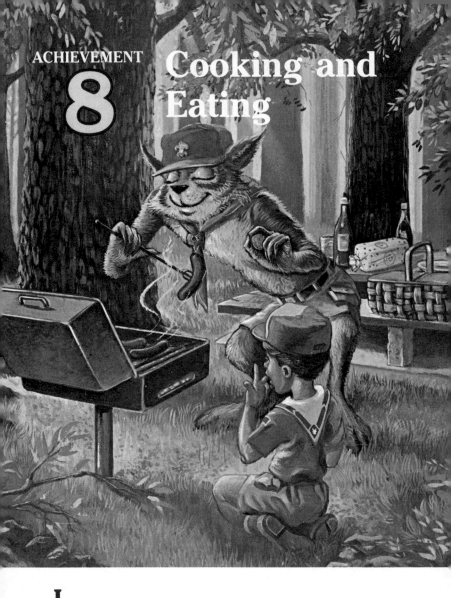

ACHIEVEMENT 8 Cooking and Eating

It's fun to be the cook. The cook fixes the meal and may or may not use a stove. You won't need a stove for sandwiches and salads.

8a. List some foods from each of the four basic food groups.

1. Fruits and vegetables
   (four servings a day)
   - ☐ _____
   - ☐ _____
   - ☐ _____
   - ☐ _____

2. Breads and cereals
   (four servings a day)
   - ☐ _____
   - ☐ _____
   - ☐ _____
   - ☐ _____

3. Dairy products
   (three servings a day)
   - ☐ _____
   - ☐ _____
   - ☐ _____

4. Proteins
   (two servings a day)
   - ☐ _____
   - ☐ _____

(a) Akela's OK   Date   Recorded by den leader

8b. Plan the meals you and your family should have for one day. List things your family should have from the four food groups.

Breakfast _____

_____

Lunch _____

_____

Dinner _____

_____

b Akela's OK   Date   Recorded by den leader

8c. Help fix at least one meal for your family. Help set the table, cook the food, and wash the dishes.

Foods, dishes, knives, forks, and spoons must be clean. If they are dirty you may get sick.

c Akela's OK   Date   Recorded by den leader

WOLF TRAIL

REQUIREMENT

8d. Fix your own breakfast. Wash and put away the dishes.

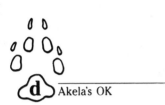

(d) Akela's OK   Date   Recorded by den leader

REQUIREMENT

8e. Help to plan, prepare, and cook an outdoor meal.

(e) Akela's OK   Date   Recorded by den leader

COOKING AND EATING   83

ACHIEVEMENT 9

Be Safe at Home and on the Street

You can be careful and safe and still have fun. It's a lot more fun if you and other people don't get hurt. Let's learn how to be safe at home, and outside, too.

9a. *WITH A GROWN-UP*, check your home for things that may help keep you safe.

- Keep tools and toys in their places.

- Keep storage areas clear of waste and trash.

- Use a step stool and stepladder to reach high places.

- Be sure poisons are marked and stored where children can't get them.

- Dry your hands before touching an electric switch.

- Keep stairs clear. Help put things where they belong in closets, the attic, basement, or storeroom.

- Keep closets neat.

- Know where the water shutoff valve is.

- Know where the electric fuse box or circuit breaker box is.

Akela's OK   Date   Recorded by den leader

BE SAFE AT HOME AND ON THE STREET   85

9b. *WITH A GROWN-UP*, check for danger from fire.

- Don't play with matches.

- Ask a grown-up to keep gasoline and other dangerous things marked and away from fires or strong heat.

- Keep matches where small children cannot reach them.

- Visit a fire station to learn how you can prevent fires.

- Know where the fire exits are in all the buildings you enter. Look for EXIT signs.

- Plan a family escape route from your home. Draw a floor plan and show the ways your family can get out in case of fire.

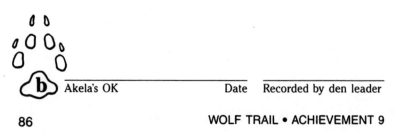

Akela's OK	Date	Recorded by den leader

9c. Practice good rules of street and road safety.

- Don't play in the street.

- Walk on the left side of the road when there is no sidewalk. Face traffic, watch out for cars.

- Obey traffic signs.

- Cross at crossings. Watch traffic and look both ways before you step into the street.

- Wear your seat belt while riding in a car.

<u>   </u>   <u>   </u>

(**C**) Akela's OK   Date   Recorded by den leader

9d. Know the rules of bike safety.

If you have to ride in the road, keep to the right.

Ride your bike in a safe place.

Watch out for others.

Watch out for drain grates.

Don't be a show-off.

WOLF TRAIL

With your left arm,
show others what
you are going to do.

Right Turn

Left Turn

Bicycle Helmet

Stop or Slow

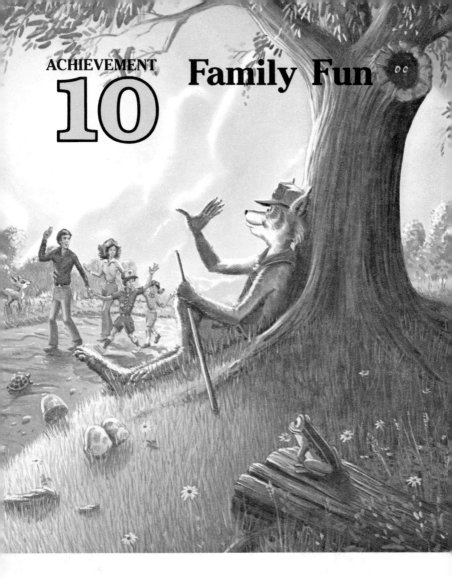

10 Family Fun

Here are some things to do that are fun for everyone. There are games to play, places to go, and things to do with your family.

DO TWO OF THESE FIVE REQUIREMENTS

10a. **Make a game like one of these. Play it with your family.**

Eagle Golf

⟵ **Tin Can**

Take turns dropping beans straight down into a small tin can. Each time a bean goes into the can is 1 point. To win, you must get as many points as you are old before the other players.

Beanbag Archery

Leader tosses beanbag out as a target. Other players try to hit it. Closest one becomes the leader for the next toss.

Bull's-eye

10b. Plan a walk. Go to a park or a wooded area, or visit a zoo or museum with your family.

We went to _____

_____

ⓑ Akela's OK   Date   Recorded by den leader

10c. Read a book or *Boys' Life* magazine with your family. Take turns reading aloud.

We read _____

_____

ⓒ Akela's OK   Date   Recorded by den leader

10d. Decide with Akela what you will watch on television or listen to on the radio.

We watched or listened to _____

_____

d Akela's OK   Date   Recorded by den leader

10e. Attend a concert, a play, or other live program with your family.

We attended _____

_____

e Akela's OK   Date   Recorded by den leader

FAMILY FUN   93

ACHIEVEMENT 11 — Duty to God

A Cub Scout promises to do his duty to God. What is your duty to God? How do you do it? Your family can help you learn about God. This will help.

REQUIREMENT
11a. **Talk with your folks about what they believe is their duty to God.**

Cub Scout Promise

I, ... , promise to do my best
(your name)
To do my duty to God and my country
To help other people, and
To obey the Law of the Pack

a Akela's OK   Date Recorded by den leader

REQUIREMENT
11b. **Give some ideas on how you can show your religious beliefs.**

_____

_____

_____

b Akela's OK   Date Recorded by den leader

DUTY TO GOD   95

11c. **Find out how you can help your church, synagogue, or religious fellowship.**

REQUIREMENT

I found out that _____

_____

_____

_____

_____

RELIGIOUS EMBLEMS PROGRAM

If you or your pack is part of a church or synagogue, you can earn the religious emblem of your own age and faith.

Metta
Buddhist

Faith in God
Church of Jesus Christ
of Latter-day Saints

Aleph
Jewish

NOTE for Akela: Ask your religious leader or council service center about the religious emblems programs available to Cub Scouts.

Akela's OK   Date   Recorded by den leader

God and Family
Lutheran

Chi Rho
Orthodox

Parvuli Dei
Roman Catholic

GOD AND ME
Protestant
Tiger Cub—
8-year-old Cub Scout

GOD AND FAMILY
Protestant
Cub Scout

World Community
Reorganized Church
of Jesus Christ of
Latter Day Saints

Silver Crest
The Salvation Army

DUTY TO GOD

ACHIEVEMENT 12

Making Choices

We have to choose things all the time. What to do. Where to go. Who to be with. This will help you learn how to make the best choices.

WOLF TRAIL • ACHIEVEMENT 12

DO FOUR OF THESE NINE REQUIREMENTS

REQUIREMENT

12a. There is an older boy who hangs around Jason's school. He tries to give pills to the children. What would you do if you were Jason?

I would _____

_____

_____

a Akela's OK   Date   Recorded by den leader

REQUIREMENT

12b. Mel is home alone. The phone rings. When Mel answers, someone asks if Mel's mother is home. She is not. Mel is alone. What would you do if you were Mel?

I would _____

_____

_____

b Akela's OK   Date   Recorded by den leader

MAKING CHOICES

12c. John is on a walk with his little sister. A car stops and a man asks them to come over to the car. What would you do if you were John?

I would _____

_____

_____

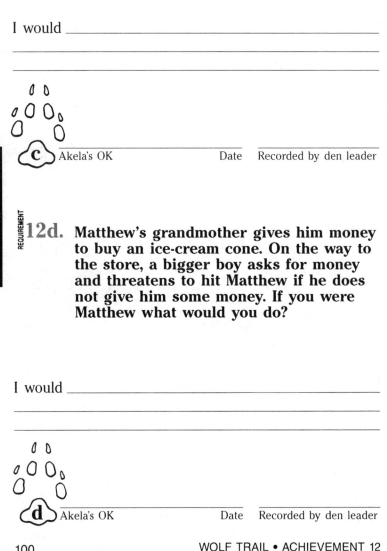

c Akela's OK   Date   Recorded by den leader

12d. Matthew's grandmother gives him money to buy an ice-cream cone. On the way to the store, a bigger boy asks for money and threatens to hit Matthew if he does not give him some money. If you were Matthew what would you do?

I would _____

_____

_____

d Akela's OK   Date   Recorded by den leader

WOLF TRAIL

12e. Chris and his little brother are home alone in the afternoon. A man knocks on the door and says he wants to read the meter. He is not wearing a uniform. What would you do if you were Chris?

I would _____

_____

_____

_e_ Akela's OK   Date   Recorded by den leader

12f. Sam is home alone. He looks out the window and sees a man trying to break into a neighbor's back door. What would you do if you were Sam?

I would _____

_____

_____

_f_ Akela's OK   Date   Recorded by den leader

MAKING CHOICES   101

REQUIREMENT

12g. **Some kids who go to Bob's school want him to steal candy and gum from a store, which they can share later. Bob knows this is wrong, but he wants to be popular with these kids. What would you do if you were Bob?**

I would _____

_____

_____

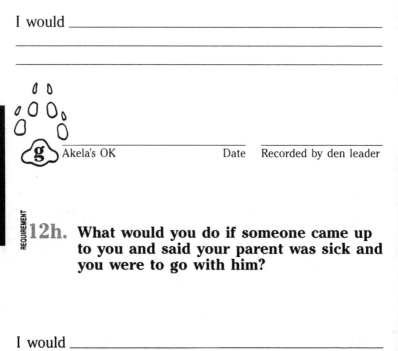

g Akela's OK   Date   Recorded by den leader

REQUIREMENT

12h. **What would you do if someone came up to you and said your parent was sick and you were to go with him?**

I would _____

_____

_____

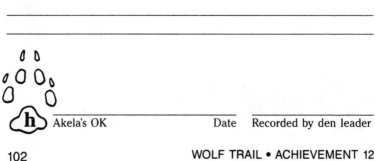

h Akela's OK   Date   Recorded by den leader

WOLF TRAIL

12i. **What would you do if you were in a public restroom and someone tried to touch you?**

I would _____

_____

_____

When you are afraid, remember:

IT IS NOT YOUR FAULT if someone tries to hurt you.

IT IS NOT YOUR FAULT if someone tries to make you feel bad.

IT IS NOT YOUR FAULT if someone tries to scare you and mix you up.

You can:

• Get away

• Say "NO"

• Yell "HELP"

• Tell someone

NOTE for Akela: Help your Cub Scout understand that you want him to feel safe and there are things he can do to protect himself.

_____   _____
Akela's OK   Date   Recorded by den leader

When you have filled in 49 of my tracks through all 12 parts of the Wolf trail, you have earned the right to wear my BADGE.

Your Wolf badge will be presented at the pack meeting.

YOU ARE NOW A

WOLF CUB SCOUT

Arrow Point Trail

NOW, you can earn a
GOLD
Arrow Point
and
SILVER
Arrow Points.

This arrow point
tells you what to do.

Fill in this arrow point
when you have done it.

For any 10 filled-in arrow points
you can get your

GOLD
Arrow Point

and 10 more your

SILVER
Arrow Point

and 10 more another

SILVER
Arrow Point

and so on

1

It's a Secret

Learn to send secret messages. Only those who know the secret can read them. Learn to "talk" with your hands.

a ▶ Use a secret code.

You can use numbers for letters.

13 25 14 11 3 5
9 19
10 9 13

1	A	14	N
2	B	15	O
3	C	16	P
4	D	17	Q
5	E	18	R
6	F	19	S
7	G	20	T
8	H	21	U
9	I	22	V
10	J	23	W
11	K	24	X
12	L	25	Y
13	M	26	Z

13	25	14	1	13	5	9	19	10	9	13	.
M	Y	N	A	M	E	I	S	J	I	M	.

23	8	1	20	9	19	25	15	21	18	19	?
W	H	A	T	I	S	Y	O	U	R	S	?

a ▽

_____ _____
Akela's OK   Date   Recorded by den leader

Or turn alphabet upside down.

A	Z
B	Y
C	X
D	W
E	V
F	U
G	T
H	S
I	R
J	Q
K	P
L	O
M	N

N	M
O	L
P	K
Q	J
R	I
S	H
T	G
U	F
V	E
W	D
X	C
Y	B
Z	A

R ZN VRTSG
I AM EIGHT

SLD LOW ZIV BLF?

DSZG RH BLFI OZHG MZNV?

My code is _____

Akela's OK   Date   Recorded by den leader

b ▸ **Write to a friend in invisible "ink."**

To make the ink, use MILK milk or

lemon juice.

Jim —
Meet me
after school
today —
Pete

Use a toothpick for a pen.

When the "ink" dries, you can't see it until you hold it over a light. The heat from the light will turn the "ink" light brown.

ARROW POINT TRAIL

b / Akela's OK _____ Date _____ Recorded by den leader

108 ARROW POINT TRAIL • ELECTIVE 1

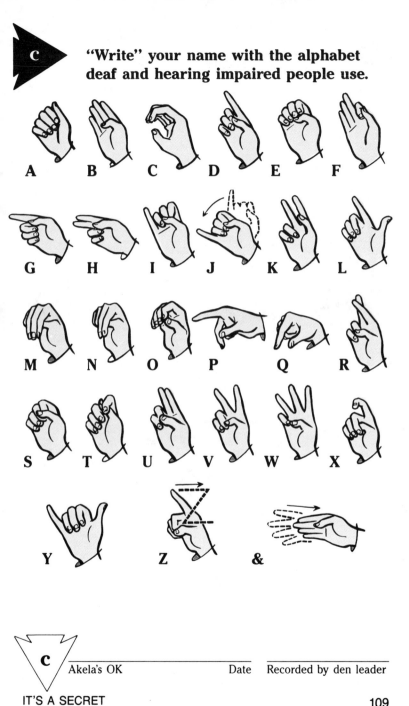

"Write" your name with the alphabet deaf and hearing impaired people use.

A B C D E F

G H I J K L

M N O P Q R

S T U V W X

Y Z &

Akela's OK   Date   Recorded by den leader

IT'S A SECRET

Use 12 Indian signs to tell a story.

INDIAN SIGN LANGUAGE

| Listen | I or Me | You or Him | Yes |

| Go | Come | Bring | Walk |

Night   Sun   Moon   Hungry

Take   Run   With   Day

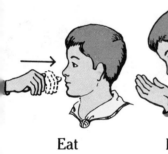

Eat   Drink   Sleep   Water

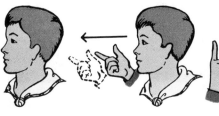

Friend   Talk   Man   Woman

Mind   Scout   Sunrise   Tongue

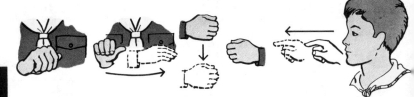

Heart   Good   Brave   True

What does this say?

for a

of

A

to Akela   then

a   !

ELECTIVE 2

Be an Actor

It's fun to be an actor. You can make believe you are anyone you want to be.

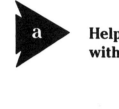

a   **Help to plan and put on a skit with costumes.**

ARROW POINT TRAIL

a   _____   _____   _____
Akela's OK   Date   Recorded by den leader

b **Make some scenery for a den skit.**

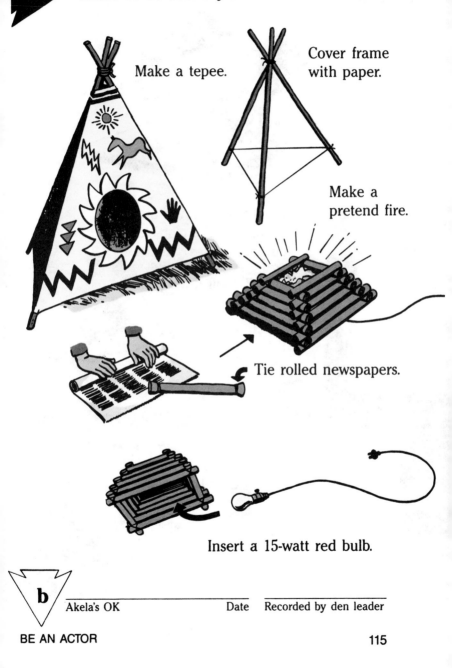

Make a tepee.

Cover frame with paper.

Make a pretend fire.

Tie rolled newspapers.

Insert a 15-watt red bulb.

Make sound effects for a den skit.

1. Pound plastic bowls on a board for the clop-clop sound of horses.

2. Roll dried peas in a pan for rain.

3. Rattle cardboard for thunder.

ARROW POINT TRAIL

4. Slap floor
   or table
   for gunshot.

5. Use a
   bicycle
   bell for a
   telephone ring.

**NOTE for Akela: Make these sounds behind a door or a screen so that the
audience will think they are real.**

BE AN ACTOR

d Be the announcer for a den skit.

d

Akela's OK   Date   Recorded by den leader

Akela's OK   Date   Recorded by den leader

Make It Yourself

Watch carpenters and craftsmen at work. Learn how to handle tools; then pick a project and do it.

a   **Make something useful for your home, church, or school.**

RECIPE CARD HOLDER

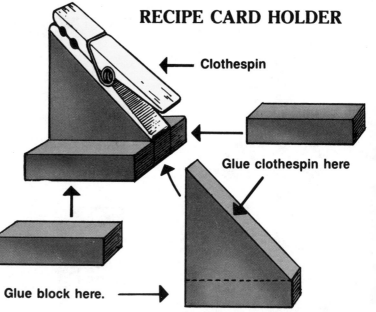

← Clothespin

Glue clothespin here

Glue block here. →

Sand the pieces smooth with sandpaper or steel wool before you put them together.

a   <u>Akela's OK</u>   Date   Recorded by den leader

A "CM" RULER

Measure to see how far you can stretch your hand.

This hand span is almost 12 CM. What's yours?

100 CM = 1 meter
Meters are used in sports.
See page 209.

CM is short for centimeter.

These spaces are ► centimeters. You may cut this out of your book. Paste it on a smooth piece of wood.

_____   _____
Akela's OK   Date   Recorded by den leader

MAKE IT YOURSELF

0
1
2
3
4
5
6
7
8
9
10
11
12
13
14
15
16
17
18

A BENCH FORK

Hold the piece on the fork and cut straight up and down with a coping saw. The fork lets you move the pieces around to cut curves.

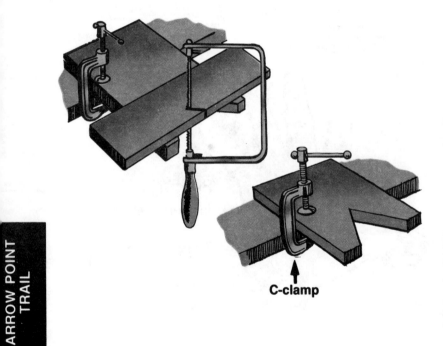

C-clamp

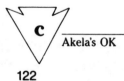

Akela's OK   Date   Recorded by den leader

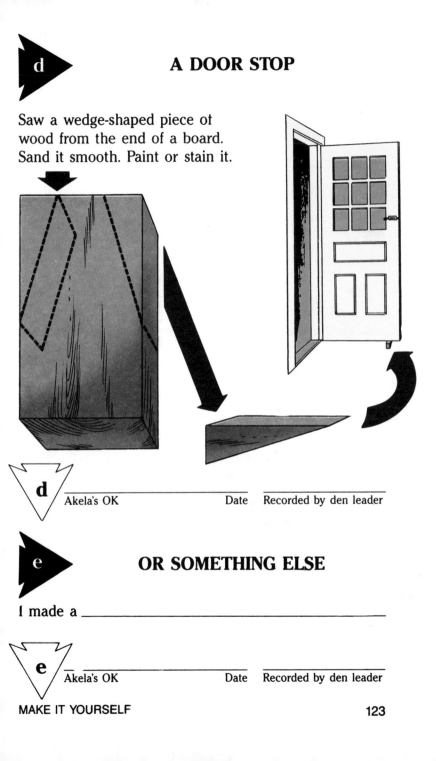

A DOOR STOP

Saw a wedge-shaped piece of wood from the end of a board. Sand it smooth. Paint or stain it.

d _____ _____ _____
Akela's OK   Date   Recorded by den leader

OR SOMETHING ELSE

I made a _____

e _____ _____ _____
Akela's OK   Date   Recorded by den leader

ELECTIVE 4

Play a Game

Play these games with children younger than you are, with other Cub Scouts, or with grown-ups.

▶ **a**　**Play Pie-tin Washer Toss**

Each player tosses five washers at a pie tin. Score one point for each washer that stays in pan.

▽
a _____　_____
　　Akela's OK　　　　　　　Date　　Recorded by den leader

▶ **b**　**Play Marble Sharpshooter**

Each player rolls five marbles at soda-bottle targets. Score one point for each marble that rolls between bottles and misses them.

▽
b _____　_____
　　Akela's OK　　　　　　　Date　　Recorded by den leader

ARROW POINT TRAIL

Play Ring Toss

Make five rings out of rope, rubber, wire, heavy cardboard or folded newspaper.

Toss at stick in the ground or on a stand.

Ringers = 3 points
Leaners = 1 point

d Play Beanbag Toss

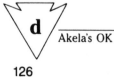

Make a target out of heavy cardboard. Color it. Each player throws five beanbags. Score three points for hitting the eyes, one point for the mouth.

Fold

Fold

Tape

d

Akela's OK   Date   Recorded by den leader

Play a Game of Marbles

Put marbles in a circle like this.

Stand behind the pitch line and toss your shot toward the lag line.

Player nearest the lag line shoots first from the edge of the circle.

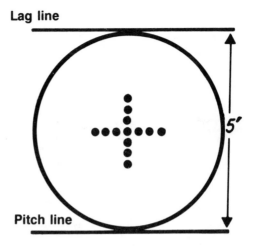

Lag line

5'

Pitch line

First player to knock seven marbles out of the circle is the winner.

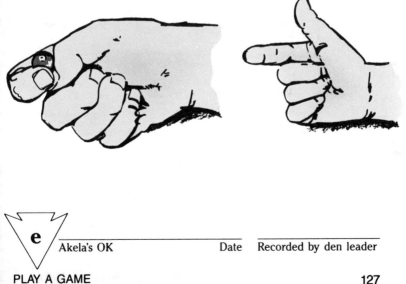

ELECTIVE 5 **Sparetime Fun**

Ride the wind and waves with kites and boats you can make yourself.

 a **Explain safety rules for kite flying.**

Fly kites away from electrical wires.

Fly kites in fair weather.
Put them away if a storm approaches.

Make kites with paper and wood,
never metal—it might
attract lightning.

Use dry string for kite line.

Fly kites in an open field or park,
never on a street or railroad line.

If a kite gets caught in wires, a treetop,
or somewhere else, have your parent or
another adult see if it can be saved.

Remember, have fun but play it safe.

ARROW POINT TRAIL

a —————————————————— ——————————————
　Akela's OK　　　　　　　　Date　　Recorded by den leader

Make and fly a kite.

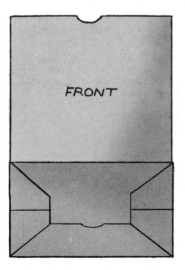

Make a paper-bag kite.

All you need for this kite
is a big paper bag and
some tape and string.

FRONT

1. Cut out the
   bottom of the
   bag. Fold
   down the
   sides and
   make the
   bag flat.

2. Turn the bag over. Make a mark in the center of the bag a third of the way down. Draw lines to the corners and cut out the pieces on this side.

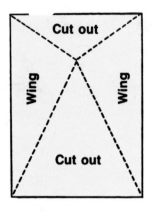

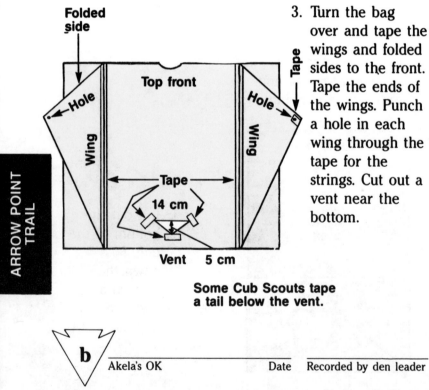

3. Turn the bag over and tape the wings and folded sides to the front. Tape the ends of the wings. Punch a hole in each wing through the tape for the strings. Cut out a vent near the bottom.

Some Cub Scouts tape a tail below the vent.

b

_____

Akela's OK   Date   Recorded by den leader

c   **OR make a two-stick kite.**

1.

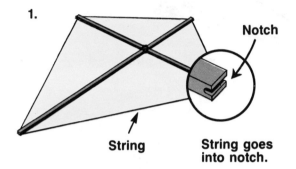

Notch

String

String goes into notch.

2.

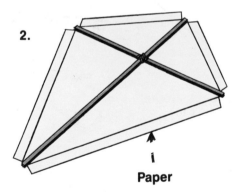

Paper

Fold paper over string and paste.

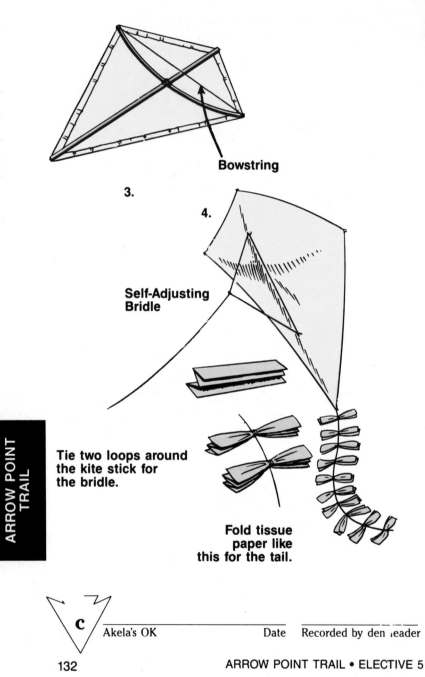

Bowstring

3.

4.

Self-Adjusting Bridle

Tie two loops around the kite stick for the bridle.

Fold tissue paper like this for the tail.

Akela's OK   Date   Recorded by den leader

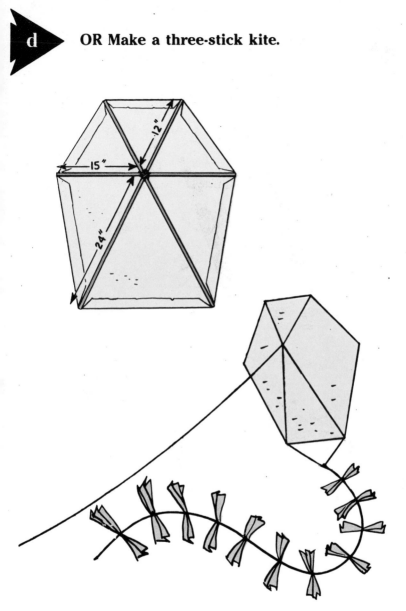

e ▶ Make and use a reel for kite string.

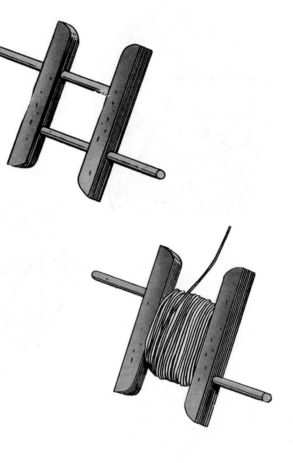

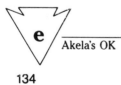

e

_____   _____
Akela's OK   Date   Recorded by den leader

**Make a model boat with a
rubber-band propeller.**

Make two holes in the propeller.
Thread the rubber band through
one hole and out the other.
Attach it to the boat. Wind it up,
and let it go!

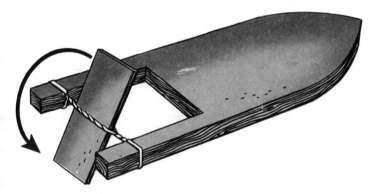

Wind the propeller this way
to make your boat go forward.

Akela's OK   Date   Recorded by den leader

ghi **Make or put together some kind of model boat.**

You can get credit each time you make a different model boat.

ARROW POINT TRAIL

g _____ Akela's OK   Date   Recorded by den leader

h _____ Akela's OK   Date   Recorded by den leader

i _____ Akela's OK   Date   Recorded by den leader

ELECTIVE 6 Books, Books, Books

Books are magical. They are the spaceships of our minds. With them you can go anywhere.

a ▶ Go to a public library with a grown-up. Find out how to get your own library card. Name four kinds of books that interest you (for example, history, science fiction, how-to books).

WESTPORT
PUBLIC
LIBRARY
Bob Bell
9 High St.
Westport, Cr.
EXPIRES MAR. 6 '89

Kinds of books that interest me:

1. _____
2. _____
3. _____
4. _____

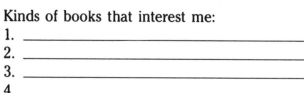

a

Akela's OK   Date   Recorded by den leader

ARROW POINT TRAIL

Choose a book on a subject you like and read it. With an adult, discuss what you read and what you think about.

c Books are important. Show that you know how to take care of them. Open a new book the right way. Make a paper or plastic cover for it or another book.

1. Hold the book on a table.

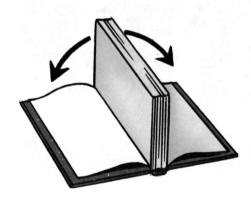

2. Let go of one cover and then the other. Put the covers down gently. Keep the pages closed and upright. Now take a few pages at a time and lightly press them down.

ARROW POINT TRAIL

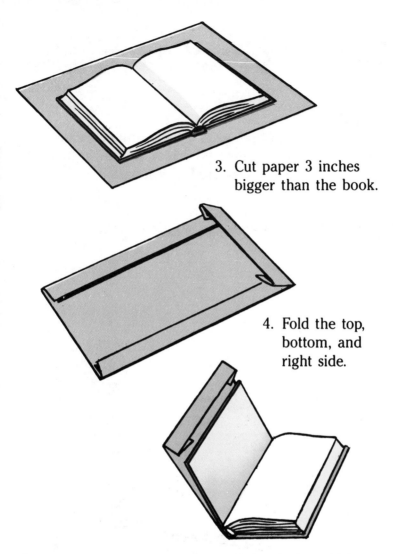

3. Cut paper 3 inches bigger than the book.

4. Fold the top, bottom, and right side.

5. Slip the book cover into the right-side fold. Make a fold for the front cover. Open the book and slip the front cover into the fold.

ELECTIVE 7 Foot Power

Foot power is a balancing act. Can you walk when your feet are off the ground? It's not as hard as it looks!

 a   **Learn to walk on a pair of stilts.**

Stand on something to get started.

ARROW POINT TRAIL

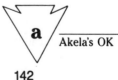

a _____
Akela's OK   Date   Recorded by den leader

b Make a pair of "puddle jumpers" and walk with them.

c Learn to ski.

FOOT POWER   143

ELECTIVE 8 Machine Power

Learn about machines. A stick can be used as a lever, a log can be used as a wheel or a roller. Talk to workers who use levers and wheels everyday.

a Name 10 kinds of trucks, construction machinery, or farm machinery.

I saw these machines:

_____   _____
_____   _____
_____   _____
_____   _____
_____   _____

NOTE for Akela: Encourage your Cub Scout to find pictures of machinery in newspapers and magazines. He can cut them out and paste them on these pages.

a _____ _____ _____
Akela's OK   Date   Recorded by den leader

MACHINE POWER   145

b Use a wheel and axle.

Any cart has wheels and axles.

Most of the load is on the axle. You can move it on the wheel.

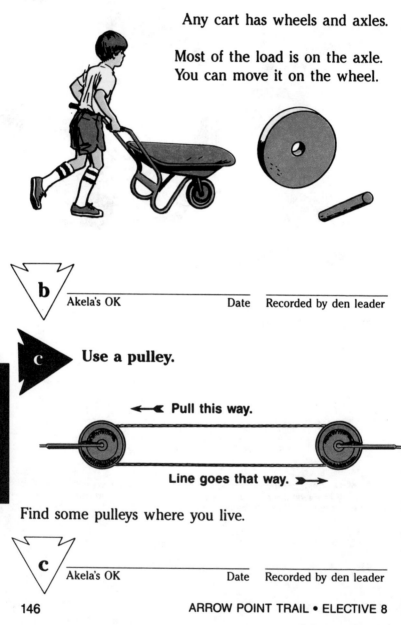

b _____ _____ _____
Akela's OK   Date   Recorded by den leader

c Use a pulley.

◄── **Pull this way.**

Line goes that way. ►──

Find some pulleys where you live.

c _____ _____ _____
Akela's OK   Date   Recorded by den leader

d ▶ **Make and use a windlass.**

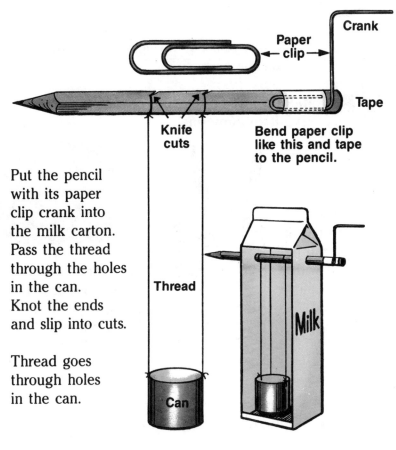

Crank

Paper
← clip →

Tape

Knife cuts

Bend paper clip like this and tape to the pencil.

Put the pencil with its paper clip crank into the milk carton. Pass the thread through the holes in the can. Knot the ends and slip into cuts.

Thread goes through holes in the can.

Thread

Milk

Can

Cut one side from a milk carton. Punch holes for the pencil.

---

d ‾‾‾‾‾‾‾‾‾‾‾‾‾‾‾‾‾   ‾‾‾‾‾‾‾ ‾‾‾‾‾‾‾‾‾‾‾‾‾‾‾‾‾

Akela's OK   Date   Recorded by den leader

ELECTIVE 9

Let's Have a Party

Parties are more fun when you've made a gift yourself and helped plan and put on the party.

a-b Make a gift or toy like one of these and give it to someone.

Beanbag

Tin-can pencil holder can be covered with string or paper and glued to the can.

Use scrap cloth or an old pocket. Fill with dried beans. Fold in the top and sew it shut.

NOTE for Akela: This gift can be given to a friend, a parent, or anyone in a hospital or retirement home. Elective credit may be given for each gift made.

a _____ _____
Akela's OK   Date   Recorded by den leader

b _____ _____
Akela's OK   Date   Recorded by den leader

Help with a home or den party.

Here are some of the things I did:

_____

_____

I helped decorate the room with

_____

_____

I helped plan and play these games.

_____

_____

I helped serve refreshments.
We had _____

_____

I helped clean up afterward by

_____

_____

Akela's OK   Date   Recorded by den leader

LET'S HAVE A PARTY   149

ELECTIVE

10

American Indian Lore

Indians were the first Americans. The more you know about them, the more you will know about America.

a ▶ **Read a book or tell a story about Indians.**

I read or told a story about _____

_____

a

Akela's OK   Date   Recorded by den leader

150   ARROW POINT TRAIL • ELECTIVE 10

ARROW POINT TRAIL

b ▶ **Make an Indian tom-tom.**

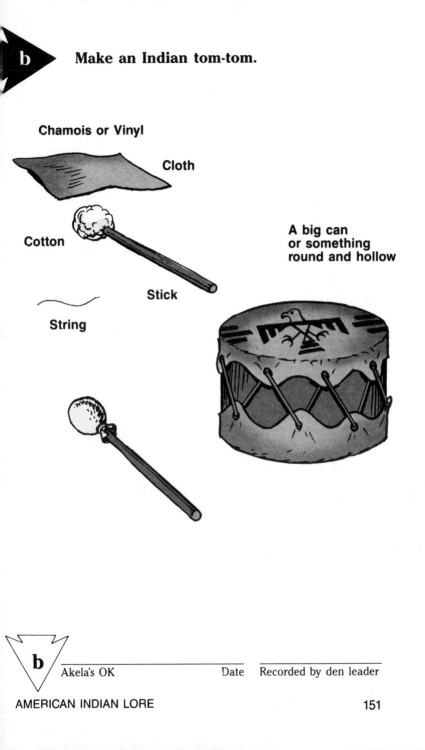

Chamois or Vinyl

Cloth

Cotton

Stick

String

A big can or something round and hollow

c ▸ **Make an Indian costume.**

◀ **Woodland Indian vest**

Plains Indian breechcloth ▶

Northwest Coast Indian hat ⬇

Southwest Hopi Indian eagle dance costume ▶

c

_____   _____   _____
Akela's OK   Date   Recorded by den leader

**Finish a feather for a headband
or other decoration.**

Use a feather about 10 inches long,
and two feather fluffs.

Glue a 2-inch strip
of thin leather to the quill,
or wrap with tape.

Glue the base fluff
to the big feather.

Wrap and glue a 2-inch
by 1-inch piece of red
felt around base of feather.

Wrap yellow thread or yarn
around the red felt and tie.

e ▶ Make a headband for the finished feather.

Use a strip of leather or vinyl long enough to go around your head and overlap an inch.

Punch two holes in the overlap to match those of the leather circle. Put feather between circle and band. Pull tight and tie inside.

e _____   _____ _____
   Akela's OK   Date   Recorded by den leader

Learn 12 word pictures and write a story with them.

Big voice

Bear alive

Bear dead

Bad

Top man

Camp

Brothers

Make peace

Council

Talk

Wise man

Hunt

| Morning | Noon | Evening | Directions |

| Man | Woman | Boy | Man on horse |

| Tepee | Hear | Spirit | Birds | Eat |

Deer	Beaver	Horses	River	Lake

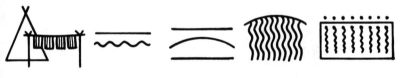

Three days	Three nights	Hungry	Fear	Look	Campfire

Food	Stormy	Clear	Rain	Cold, Snow

ELECTIVE
11

Sing-along

Learn to sing lots of songs. There are glad songs and sad songs, and some are proud like "The Star-Spangled Banner."

 a ▶ **Learn and sing the first and last verses of "America."**

America

My country, 'tis of thee,
Sweet land of liberty,
Of thee I sing;
Land where my fathers died,
Land of the pilgrim's pride,
From every mountainside
Let freedom ring.

Our father's God, to Thee,
Author of liberty,
To Thee we sing;
Long may our land be bright
With freedom's holy light,
Protect us by Thy might
Great God, our King.

ARROW POINT TRAIL

▽
a

_____   _____ _____
Akela's OK   Date   Recorded by den leader

Learn and sing the first verse of our national anthem.

The Star-Spangled Banner

O say, can you see
  by the dawn's early light
What so proudly we hailed,
  at the twilight's last gleaming,
Whose broad stripes and bright stars,
  through the perilous fight,
O'er the ramparts we watched,
  were so gallantly streaming?
And the rocket's red glare,
  the bombs bursting in air,
Gave proof through the night
  that our flag was still there!
O say, does that star-spangled
  banner yet wave
O'er the land of the free
  and the home of the brave?

b | _____ | _____ | _____
   | Akela's OK | Date | Recorded by den leader

c Learn the words and sing
three Cub Scout songs.

You can find other songs in
the *Cub Scout Songbook.*

Good Night, Cub Scouts
Tune: "Good Night, Ladies"

Good night, Cub Scouts
Good night, Cub Scouts
Good night, Cub Scouts,
We're going to leave you now.

Merrily, we Cub along, Cub along, Cub along.
Merrily, we Cub along up the Cub Scout trail.

Sweet dreams, Cub Scouts.
Sweet dreams, Cub Scouts.
Sweet dreams, Cub Scouts,
We're going to leave you now.

I Have a Dog
Tune: "Reuben, Reuben, I've Been Thinking"

I have a dog, his name is Fido,
I have raised him from a pup.
He can stand upon his hind legs
If you hold his front legs up!

ARROW POINT TRAIL

Train Song

Tune: "Yankee Doodle"

I met an engine on a hill
All hot and broken-hearted,
And this is what he said to me
As up the hill he started.

(Slowly)

I think I can, I think I can
At any rate, I'll try.
I think I can, I think I can
At any rate, I'll try.

He reached the top, and looking back
To where he stood and doubted,
He started on the downward track
And this is what he shouted:

(Faster)

I knew I could, I knew I could,
I never should have doubted.
I knew I could, I knew I could,
I never should have doubted!

I learned _____

_____

_____

C _____   _____
Akela's OK   Date   Recorded by den leader

SING-ALONG   161

d Learn the words and sing the first verse of three other songs, hymns, or prayers. Write the verse of one of the songs learned.

_____

_____

_____

_____

_____

_____

_____

_____

_____

_____

_____

_____

_____

_____

_____

_____

_____

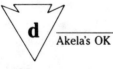

Akela's OK   Date   Recorded by den leader

Learn a song that would be sung as a grace before meals. Write the words here.

_____

_____

_____

_____

_____

_____

_____

_____

_____

_____

_____

_____

_____

_____

_____

_____

_____

_____

_____

_____

e /
Akela's OK   Date   Recorded by den leader

Be an Artist

ELECTIVE

You can't tell if you can draw a picture until you try. Someday, you may become an artist or a draftsman.

a ▶ **Make a freehand sketch.**

Draw anything you like here.

a _____ _____
Akela's OK   Date   Recorded by den leader

ARROW POINT TRAIL

Tell a story in three steps by drawing three cartoons.

c Mix yellow and blue paints to make green; yellow and red to make orange; and red and blue to make violet.

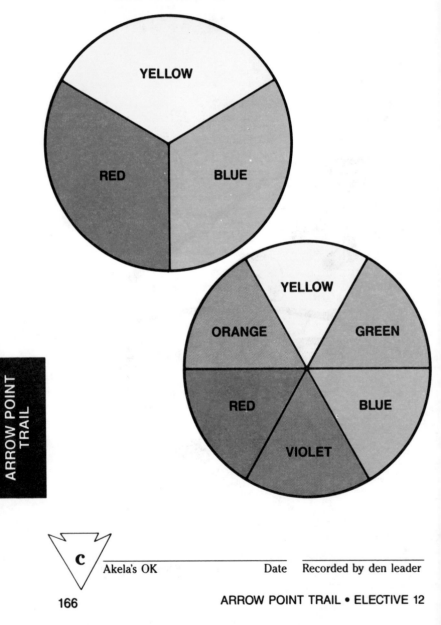

ARROW POINT TRAIL

d Help draw, paint, or crayon some scenery for a den or pack skit or puppet show.

Use a large sheet of paper or cardboard.

City

Country

d _____   _____
Akela's OK   Date   Recorded by den leader

BE AN ARTIST   167

Make a stencil pattern.

Draw

Use heavy paper.
Cut out the parts
that will be painted.
Place them on a sheet
of paper and paint.

Cut out

Paint

e

Akela's OK   Date   Recorded by den leader

Make a poster for a Cub Scout project or pack meeting.

ELECTIVE 13

Birds

Some birds follow the sun each year. These summer visitors need homes. The ones that stay behind need to be fed.

a Make a list of all the birds you saw in a week and tell where you saw them (field, forest, marsh, yard, or park).

_____

_____

_____

_____

_____

_____

_____

_____

_____

_____

_____

_____

ARROW POINT TRAIL

a

Akela's OK   Date   Recorded by den leader

b Put out nesting material (yarn and string) for birds and tell which birds might use it.

b _____ _____
Akela's OK   Date   Recorded by den leader

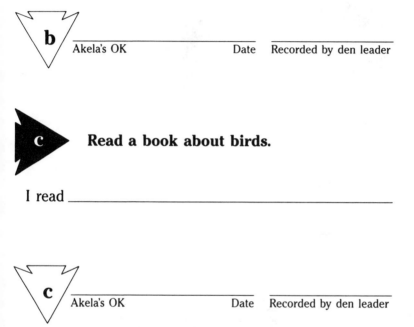

c Read a book about birds.

I read _____

c _____ _____
Akela's OK   Date   Recorded by den leader

d Point out 10 different kinds of birds (5 may be from pictures).

d _____ _____
Akela's OK   Date   Recorded by den leader

Feed wild birds and tell which birds you fed.

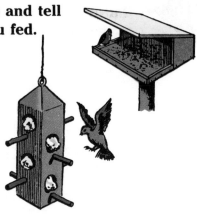

Feed birds all winter.

Birds like bread crumbs, cracked corn, sunflower seeds, millet, or other grains.

Make your own birdbath.

Keep the birdbath clean.

Garbage can top

Piece of broomstick

2×4s

e

_____ _____
Akela's OK   Date   Recorded by den leader

**Put out a birdhouse and tell
which birds use it.**

Lift top to clean.

Clean the birdhouse each year in the fall.

ELECTIVE

14

Pets

Your pet may be a dog, cat, rabbit, parakeet, or a tropical fish.
All pets need care—even
crickets.

a   **Take care of a pet.**

Dogs need a clean place to
live. Feed your dog dog food
and water. Don't feed your dog
small bones.

ARROW POINT
TRAIL

Keep your rabbit hutch clean.
Feed your rabbit pellets.

Feed your bird birdseed, grit, and water.

Keep the cage clean.

Gerbils, hamsters, guinea pigs, white mice, and rats need prepared food, nuts, seeds, and water. Clean the cage everyday.

Cats are good companions. Give them cat food, not table scraps—they contain too much fat and starch. Always keep fresh water available.

PETS

Feed fish prepared fish food, lettuce, cabbage, or celery leaves.

My pet is a _____

Its name is _____

This is what I do to take care of it:

_____
_____
_____
_____
_____

a _____   _____   _____
Akela's OK   Date   Recorded by den leader

Know what to do when you meet a strange dog.

If a dog comes up to you:

1. Stand still with your hands down. Let the dog sniff them.

2. Don't make any quick moves and don't pet him

3. Don't try to scare him away or show that you are afraid.

4. Walk away quietly. **Don't run.**

b

Akela's OK   Date Recorded by den leader

PETS

Read a book about a pet and tell about it at a den meeting.

I read _____

c

Akela's OK   Date   Recorded by den leader

d

**Tell what is meant by rabid. Tell what
you should do if you see a dog
or wild animal that acts
as if it may be rabid.**

Rabid means **SICK!**

Don't go near
wild animals that
seem to be **TAME.**

Don't go near a dog
that seems to be—

CHOKING

EXCITED

AFRAID

Tell a grown-up right away if you are bitten
or scratched by any pet or wild animal.

ELECTIVE 15

Grow Something

Growing a garden is almost like magic. You put tiny seeds into the ground, and presto, little green plants spring up.

 a ▶ **Plant and raise a box garden.**

Put stones in the bottom and soil on the top. Pour water into the pipe.

a ▽ _____
Akela's OK   Date   Recorded by den leader

Plant and raise a flower bed.

I grew _____

Grow a plant indoors.

Pineapple   Grapefruit   Mimosa   Avocado   Sweet potato

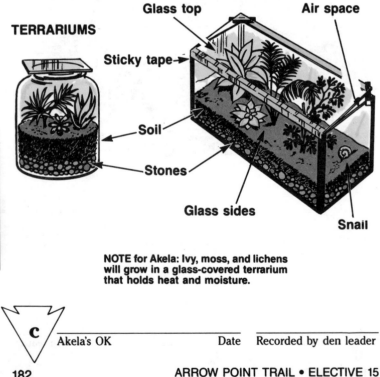

TERRARIUMS

Glass top

Air space

Sticky tape

Soil

Stones

Glass sides

Snail

NOTE for Akela: Ivy, moss, and lichens will grow in a glass-covered terrarium that holds heat and moisture.

c

_____   _____
Akela's OK   Date   Recorded by den leader

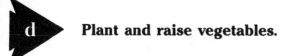

Plant and raise vegetables.

Do this on your own or with your family or den.

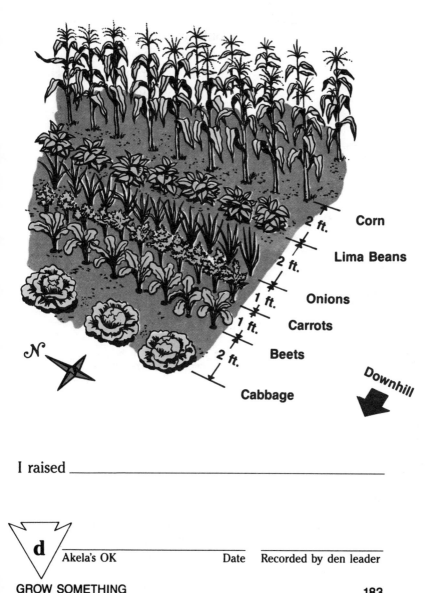

2 ft. **Corn**

2 ft. **Lima Beans**

1 ft. **Onions**

1 ft. **Carrots**

2 ft. **Beets**

Cabbage

Downhill

I raised _____

ELECTIVE 16

Family Alert

Would you know what to do if your home was hit by a tornado, flood, or hurricane? Here are three things you can do.

a ▶ **Talk with your family about what you will do in an emergency.**

In case of a fire we will _____

_____

_____

My job is to _____

_____

NOTE for Akela: Guide your son in this project, depending upon your own home, needs, and types of emergencies in your area.

a _____   _____
  Akela's OK   Date   Recorded by den leader

b ▶ **In case of a bad storm or flood, know where you can get safe food and water in your home. Tell how to purify water. Show one way. Know where and how to shut off water, electricity, gas, or oil.**

I purified water by _____

_____

We have emergency food and clothing in the _____

_____

NOTE for Akela: Boil water for 5 minutes. Ask a health officer for other methods. Tell your Cub Scout where he can get safe food and water in an emergency.

b _____   _____
Akela's OK   Date   Recorded by den leader

c **Make a list of your first aid supplies, or make a first aid kit. Know where the first aid things are kept.**

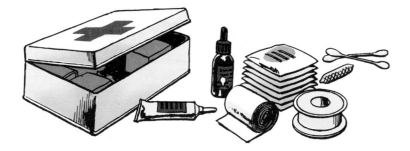

c _____   _____
Akela's OK   Date   Recorded by den leader

FAMILY ALERT   185

Tie It Right

Do your shoes come untied all by themselves? Maybe the knots you tie are to blame.

a **Learn to tie an overhand knot and a square knot.**

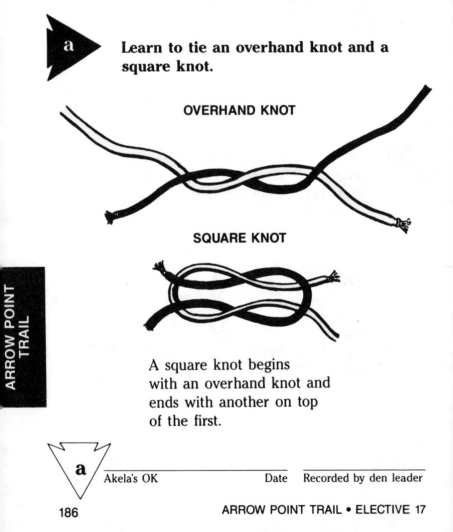

OVERHAND KNOT

SQUARE KNOT

A square knot begins with an overhand knot and ends with another on top of the first.

a Akela's OK _____ Date _____ Recorded by den leader

ARROW POINT TRAIL

Tie your shoelaces with a square bow knot.

1

2

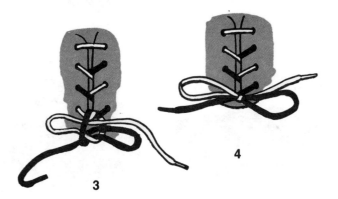

3

4

c **Wrap and tie a package so that it is neat and tight.**

1. Make a neat pile of things on the paper.

2. Fold over the long sides of the paper. Fold in the ends.

3. Go once around and cross over the string.

4. Flip over and tie with a square knot.

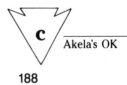

c _____   _____
Akela's OK   Date   Recorded by den leader

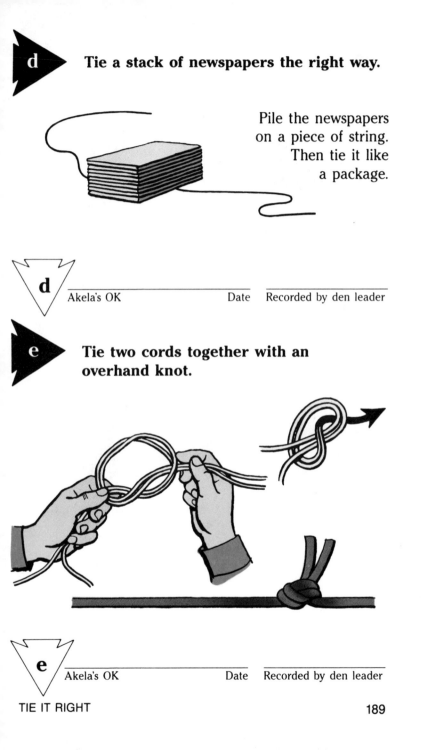

d ▶ Tie a stack of newspapers the right way.

Pile the newspapers on a piece of string. Then tie it like a package.

d / ‾‾‾‾‾‾‾‾‾‾‾‾‾‾‾‾‾‾‾‾‾‾ ‾‾‾‾‾‾‾‾‾‾‾‾‾‾‾‾
Akela's OK   Date   Recorded by den leader

e ▶ Tie two cords together with an overhand knot.

e / ‾‾‾‾‾‾‾‾‾‾‾‾‾‾‾‾‾‾‾‾‾‾ ‾‾‾‾‾‾‾‾‾‾‾‾‾‾‾‾
Akela's OK   Date   Recorded by den leader

f Learn to tie a necktie.

1   2   3

4   5   6

ARROW POINT TRAIL

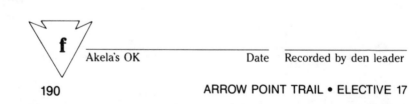

f

Akela's OK   Date   Recorded by den leader

g Wrap the end of a rope with tape to keep it from unwinding.

TWISTED ROPE

BRAIDED ROPE

18

Outdoor Adventure

A lot of Cub Sc**outing** belongs outdoors with picnics, treasure hunts, and adventure trails.

a Help plan and hold a picnic with your family or den.

a
‾‾‾‾‾‾‾‾‾‾‾‾‾‾‾‾‾‾‾‾‾‾‾‾   ‾‾‾‾‾‾‾‾‾‾‾‾‾‾‾‾‾‾
Akela's OK   Date   Recorded by den leader

b With your folks, help plan and run a family or den outing.

ARROW POINT TRAIL

b
‾‾‾‾‾‾‾‾‾‾‾‾‾‾‾‾‾‾‾‾‾‾‾‾   ‾‾‾‾‾‾‾‾‾‾‾‾‾‾‾‾‾‾
Akela's OK   Date   Recorded by den leader

c ▶ **Help plan and lay out a treasure hunt something like this.**

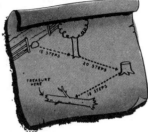

I hid my treasure _____

_____

_____

c ⟍ _____   _____
     Akela's OK   Date   Recorded by den leader

d ▶ **Help plan and lay out an obstacle race. Use this idea or make up your own.**

- Jump across an imaginary river.
- Crawl through a cardboard tunnel.
- Jump up and ring a bell.
- Toss a ball into a can.
- Do one forward roll.
- Walk like an elephant for five steps.

This is what I did: _____

_____

_____

d ⟍ _____   _____
     Akela's OK   Date   Recorded by den leader

OUTDOOR ADVENTURE   193

Help plan and lay out an adventure trail.

In a park or playground, set up five games scattered around the park. Here are five examples.

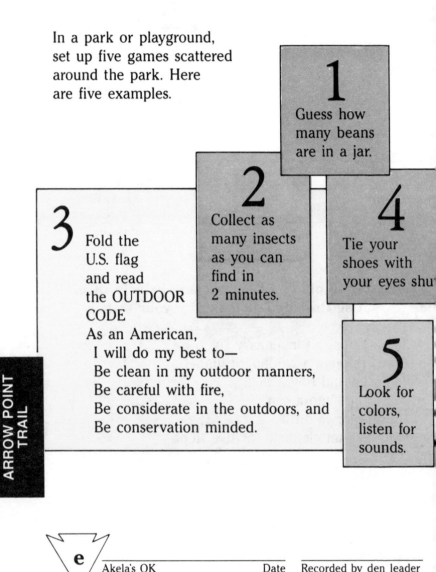

1 Guess how many beans are in a jar.

2 Collect as many insects as you can find in 2 minutes.

3 Fold the U.S. flag and read the OUTDOOR CODE

As an American,
I will do my best to—
Be clean in my outdoor manners,
Be careful with fire,
Be considerate in the outdoors, and
Be conservation minded.

4 Tie your shoes with your eyes shut

5 Look for colors, listen for sounds.

ARROW POINT TRAIL

e

_____   _____
Akela's OK   Date   Recorded by den leader

Take part in two summertime pack events with your den.

Point out poison plants. Tell what to do if you accidentally touch one of them.

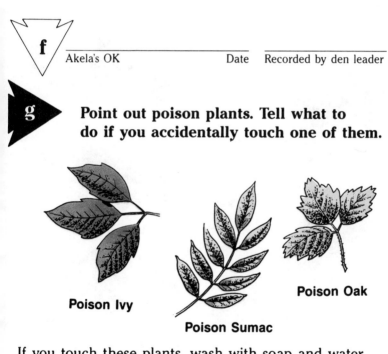

Poison Ivy

Poison Sumac

Poison Oak

If you touch these plants, wash with soap and water. Then swab with rubbing alcohol.

ELECTIVE 19

Fishing

In fishing, boys and men are equal. The fish does not know whether it's a man or a boy at the other end of the line.

a **Point out five fish.**

Here are some you might see.

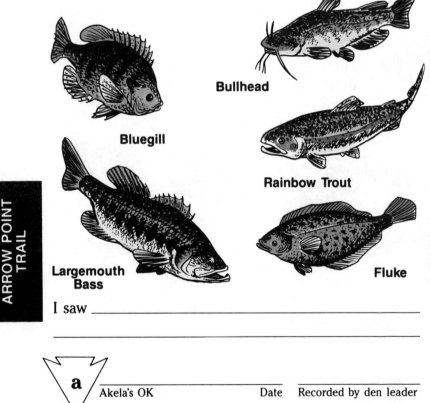

Bullhead

Bluegill

Rainbow Trout

Largemouth Bass

Fluke

I saw _____

_____

a

Akela's OK   Date   Recorded by den leader

ARROW POINT TRAIL

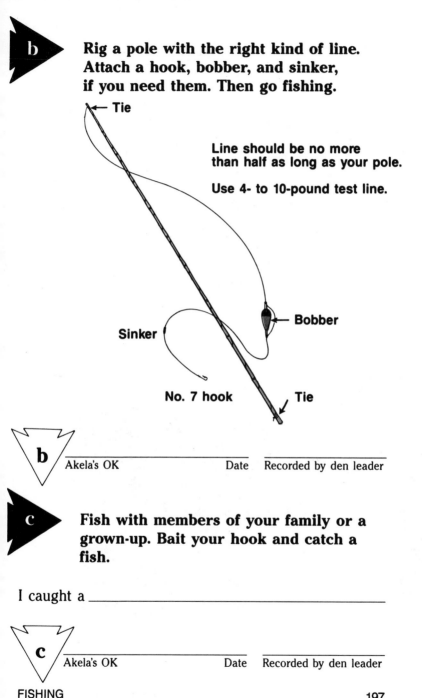

b ▶ Rig a pole with the right kind of line. Attach a hook, bobber, and sinker, if you need them. Then go fishing.

← Tie

Line should be no more than half as long as your pole.

Use 4- to 10-pound test line.

Bobber

Sinker

No. 7 hook

Tie

b Akela's OK _____ Date _____ Recorded by den leader

c ▶ Fish with members of your family or a grown-up. Bait your hook and catch a fish.

I caught a _____

c Akela's OK _____ Date _____ Recorded by den leader

d Know the rules of safe fishing.

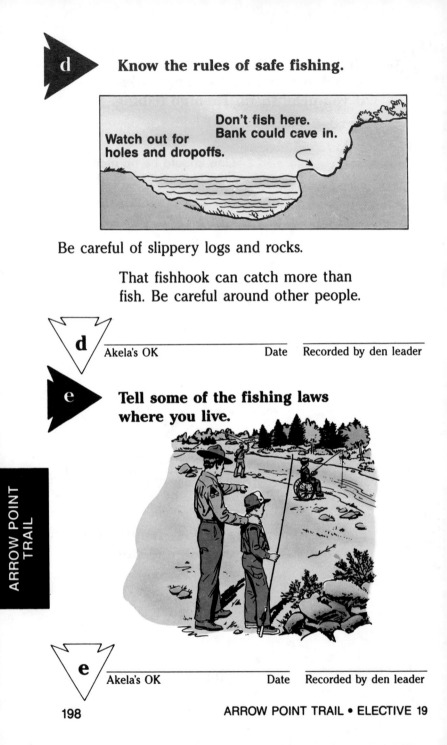

Don't fish here.
Bank could cave in.

Watch out for
holes and dropoffs.

Be careful of slippery logs and rocks.

That fishhook can catch more than
fish. Be careful around other people.

d _____   _____
Akela's OK   Date   Recorded by den leader

e Tell some of the fishing laws
where you live.

e _____   _____
Akela's OK   Date   Recorded by den leader

ARROW POINT
TRAIL

Show how to use a rod and reel.

1. Hold line with finger.

> 2. Cast rod forward, let up on the line with your finger. When the lure is where you want it, stop the reel by pressing on its edge with a finger.

> 3. Be sure you have plenty of room.

4. Reel in slowly. If you get a strike, play the fish and land it.

5. If you don't get a strike, reel in the line and cast again.

NOTE for Akela: Cub Scouts should have proper instruction in using rods and reels. Point out safety measures. Adults should go fishing with them.

f

_____   _____
Akela's OK   Date   Recorded by den leader

FISHING

ELECTIVE

20

Sports

Before beginning this elective, discuss "sportsmanship" with Akela or another adult.*

a   **Play a game of tennis, table tennis, or badminton.**

NOTE for Akela: Find someone who knows the game to help you.

a _____   _____   _____
     Akela's OK   Date   Recorded by den leader

See page 16 of this book or the inside front cover of any Cub Scout sports book.

b ◀ Know boating safety rules.

1. Go boating only with a grown-up.

2. Don't overload the boat. Wear a life preserver.

3. Stay with the boat even if it leaks. It will keep you afloat.

4. When you see lightning or if a storm comes up, head for shore.

c Know archery safety rules. Know how to shoot right. Put four of six arrows into a 1.2-meter target that is 15 steps away from you.

ARCHERY SAFETY RULES

- When handling a bow with an arrow in it (when the arrow is "nocked"), always point the arrow in a safe direction.
- Nock the arrow only when told.
- Nock the arrow only on the firing line.
- Always point the arrow downrange toward the target.
- When not shooting, always point the arrow downward.
- Never shoot straight up in the air.
- Never shoot toward anything other than the target.
- Never shoot a bow without an arrow. You could break the bow.

NOTE for Akela: Find an archer who can help you.

c _____   _____
Akela's OK   Date   Recorded by den leader

Understand the safety and courtesy codes for skiing. Show walking and kick turn. Do climbing with side stop or herringbone. Show the snow plow or stem turn, and how to get up from a fall.

SKIER'S SAFETY AND COURTESY CODES

• Good skiers always ski under control. This means you must be able to turn and stop at will. This helps you avoid running into trees and other skiers.

• Make sure your ski binding holds your foot firmly to your ski and that your release works properly.

• Ski properly clothed and only when weather and conditions permit.

• Ski in an area that matches your abilities.

• Respect the rights of other skiers.

• Keep yourself physically fit.

• When skiing downhill and overtaking another skier, stay clear of the other person. Avoid collisions.

• When you and another skier are headed toward each other always stay to the right.

- Do not stop in the middle of a trail. If you fall or must stop, get off to the side of the trail. If your fall left a hole, a "sitzmark," fill it with loose snow.

- When entering a trail from the side, look up the trail to make sure no skier is coming down. The same holds true when you stop. Check up the slope before you continue to ski down the mountain.

- Never walk on ski trails without skis on your feet.

- Your skis should be equipped with a safety strap or spring-type prongs which grab into the snow when released.

- Read and obey all traffic signs on the ski slopes.

- When using a ski lift, do not cut into the line. Wait your turn.

NOTE for Akela: Find a skier who can help you.

d

Akela's OK   Date   Recorded by den leader

Know the safety rules for ice skating. Skate, without falling, as far as you can walk in 50 steps. Come to a stop. Show a turn from forward to backward.

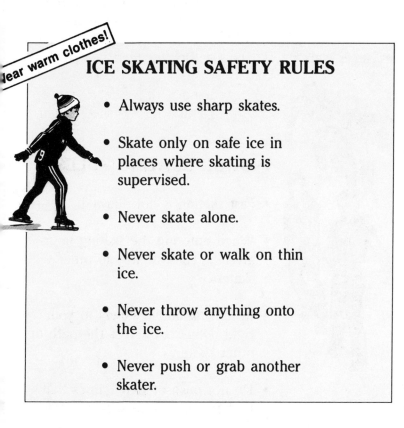

Wear warm clothes!

ICE SKATING SAFETY RULES

- Always use sharp skates.

- Skate only on safe ice in places where skating is supervised.

- Never skate alone.

- Never skate or walk on thin ice.

- Never throw anything onto the ice.

- Never push or grab another skater.

NOTE for Akela: Find a skater who can help you.

e

Akela's OK   Date   Recorded by den leader

f In roller skating, know the safety rules. From a standing start, skate forward as far as you can walk in 50 steps. Come to a stop within 10 walking steps. Skate around a corner one way without coasting. Then do the same coming back. Show a turn from forward to backward.

INDOOR SKATING RULES

• Fast skating is not allowed.

• When entering the skating floor, give the right of way to other skaters.

• In leaving, move slowly to your right. Don't cut across the path of other skaters.

• Do not push or play games that bother other skaters.

• Skate only in the direction of the skating traffic.

NOTE for Akela: Find someone who knows the game to help you.

OUTDOOR SKATING RULES

- On sidewalks, give walkers the right of way.

- Don't race out of driveways or alleys.

- Avoid skating on rough pavement.

- Don't skate on other people's property without permission.

- Stop and look both ways before you cross a street.

- Obey traffic laws, signs, and signals.

- Don't skate in the street in traffic. Take off your skates and walk.

- Avoid uncontrolled coasting down hills.

- Don't hitch onto bicycles, autos, or trucks.

- Don't skate at night.

- Check your equipment before skating. Tighten nuts. Keep straps dry and well-oiled. Replace worn straps.

f

| Akela's OK | Date | Recorded by den leader |

g Go bowling.

BE A GOOD SPORT

- Wear bowling shoes.

- Choose one bowling ball and use it.

- Bowl when it's your turn.

- Stay in your approach lane.

- Step back off the approach lane when you have finished your delivery. This lets bowlers in other lanes bowl without distraction.

- Pick up the ball with both hands, one on either side of the ball to avoid pinched fingers and hands.

- Keep the ball on the ball return where it won't roll off and hurt someone.

- Check shoelaces and be sure they are tied.

- Return the bowling ball to the storage rack and rental shoes to the counter.

Show how to make a sprint start in track. Run 45 meters in 11 seconds or less.

(The distances run in the Olympic Games are measured in meters. A meter is equal to 39.37 inches.)

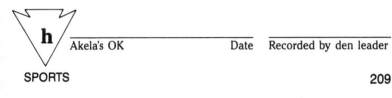

Do a 1.2-meter standing long jump.

Play a game of touch or flag football.

Fill in this arrow point if you have played a game of football or if you are a member of a football league.

NOTE for Akela: Find someone who knows the game to help you.

i

_____   _____ _____
Akela's OK   Date   Recorded by den leader

Play a game of soccer. Show how to dribble and kick.

Fill in this arrow point if you are a member of a team.

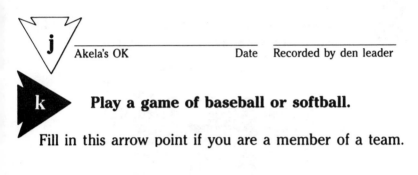

j ⁄ _____   _____
    Akela's OK   Date   Recorded by den leader

Play a game of baseball or softball.

Fill in this arrow point if you are a member of a team.

k ⁄ _____   _____
    Akela's OK   Date   Recorded by den leader

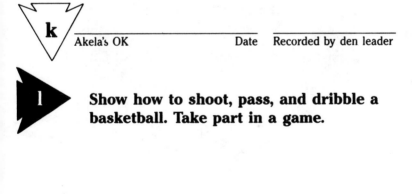

Show how to shoot, pass, and dribble a basketball. Take part in a game.

l ⁄ _____   _____
    Akela's OK   Date   Recorded by den leader

ELECTIVE 21

Computer Fun

Work is easier and play is more fun with computers.

a **Visit a place where computers are used. Find out what they are used for.**

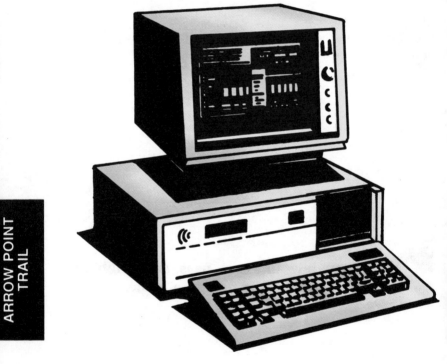

b ▶ **Play a computer game.**

▽ **b** /
‾‾‾‾‾‾‾‾‾‾‾‾‾‾‾‾‾‾‾‾‾‾‾‾‾ ‾‾‾‾‾‾‾ ‾‾‾‾‾‾‾‾‾‾‾‾‾‾‾‾‾‾‾
Akela's OK   Date   Recorded by den leader

c ▶ **Turn a computer on and off.**

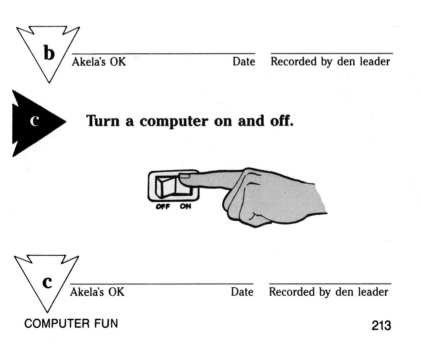

▽ **c** /
‾‾‾‾‾‾‾‾‾‾‾‾‾‾‾‾‾‾‾‾‾‾‾‾‾ ‾‾‾‾‾‾‾ ‾‾‾‾‾‾‾‾‾‾‾‾‾‾‾‾‾‾‾
Akela's OK   Date   Recorded by den leader

COMPUTER FUN   213

ELECTIVE 22

Say It Right

Being able to say what you mean is very important.

a **Say "Hello" in a language other than English.**

FRENCH *Allō*

GERMAN *Hallo*

ITALIAN *Pronto*
         Buon giorno

SPANISH *Hola*

SWAHILI *Jambo*

SWEDISH *Haj*

HEBREW *Shalom*

ARROW POINT TRAIL

a _____   _____   _____
    Akela's OK   Date   Recorded by den leader

Count to 10 in a language other than English.

	FRENCH	GERMAN	ITALIAN	SPANISH
1	Un	Eins	Uno	Uno
2	Deux	Zwei	Due	Dos
3	Trois	Drei	Tre	Tres
4	Quatre	Vier	Quattro	Cuatro
5	Cinq	Funf	Cinque	Cinco
6	Six	Sechs	Sei	Seis
7	Sept	Sieben	Sette	Siete
8	Huit	Acht	Otto	Ocho
9	Neuf	Neun	Nove	Nueve
10	Dix	Zehn	Diece	Diez

b / Akela's OK   Date   Recorded by den leader

SAY IT RIGHT   215

c Tell a short story to your den,
your den leader, or a grown-up.

Get story ideas from *Boys' Life* and other magazines.

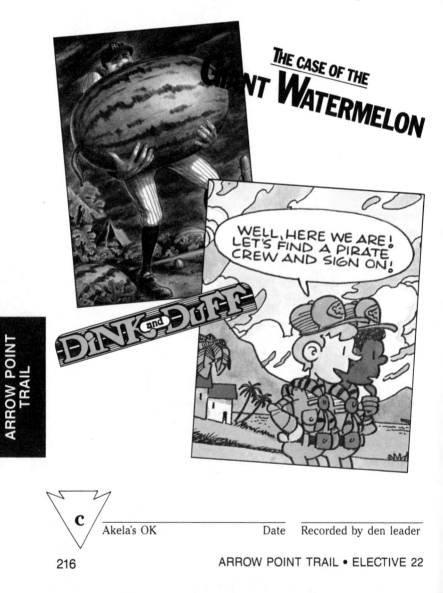

c _____ ____ _____
Akela's OK   Date   Recorded by den leader

d Tell how to get to a nearby police station from your home, your den meeting, and school. Use directions and street names.

 d _____   _____
Akela's OK   Date   Recorded by den leader

 e Invite a boy to join Cub Scouting or help a new Cub Scout through the Bobcat trail.

I invited _____

_____

_____

 **e** _____   _____
Akela's OK   Date   Recorded by den leader

Trail Summary

Your name _____

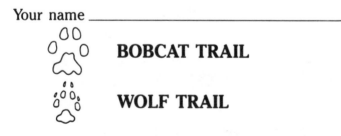

BOBCAT TRAIL

WOLF TRAIL

ARROW POINT TRAIL

NOTE for Akela: Pages 218-24 may be reproduced when more than one boy is using the book.

BOBCAT TRAIL

Fill in Seven Tracks to Earn the Bobcat Badge.

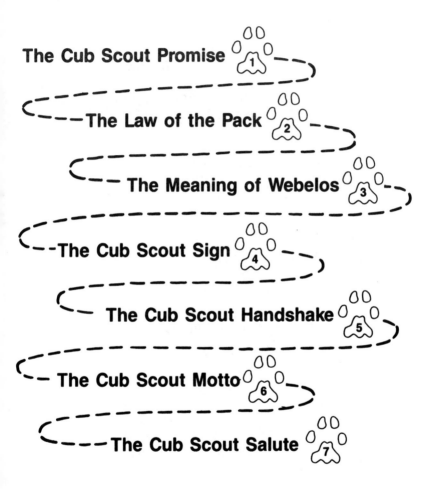

The Cub Scout Promise

The Law of the Pack

The Meaning of Webelos

The Cub Scout Sign

The Cub Scout Handshake

The Cub Scout Motto

The Cub Scout Salute

WOLF TRAIL

Fill in 49 Wolf Tracks to earn the Wolf Badge.

Achievements

Do one of these

1. Feats of Skill   (a) (b) (c) (d) (e) (f) (g) (h) (i) (j) (k)

2. Your Flag   (a) (b) (c) (d) (e)

3. Keep Your Body Healthy   (a) (b) (c)

4. Know Your Home and Community   (a) (b) (c) (d) (e)

5. Tools for Fixing and Building   (a) (b) (c) (d) (e)

6. Start a Collection   (a) (b)

7. Your Living World   ⓐ ⓑ ⓒ ⓓ ⓔ

8. Cooking and Eating   ⓐ ⓑ ⓒ ⓓ ⓔ

9. Be Safe at Home and on the Street   ⓐ ⓑ ⓒ ⓓ

Do two of these

10. Family Fun   ⓐ ⓑ ⓒ ⓓ ⓔ

11. Duty to God   ⓐ ⓑ ⓒ

Do four of these

12. Making Choices   ⓐ ⓑ ⓒ ⓓ ⓔ ⓕ ⓖ ⓗ ⓘ

ARROW POINT TRAIL

Fill in 10 Arrow Points to Earn a Gold Arrow Point.
Fill in 10 additional Arrow Points
to earn EACH Silver Arrow Point.

Electives

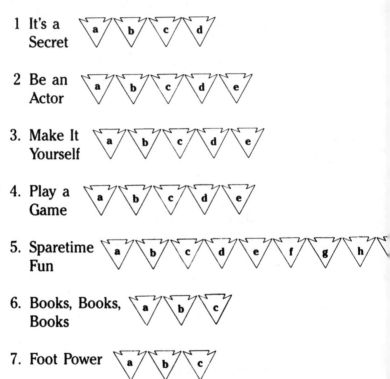

1 It's a Secret — a b c d

2 Be an Actor — a b c d e

3. Make It Yourself — a b c d e

4. Play a Game — a b c d e

5. Sparetime Fun — a b c d e f g h

6. Books, Books, Books — a b c

7. Foot Power — a b c

8. Machine Power 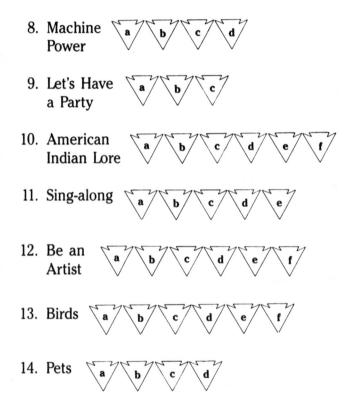 a b c d

9. Let's Have a Party a b c

10. American Indian Lore a b c d e f

11. Sing-along a b c d e

12. Be an Artist a b c d e f

13. Birds a b c d e f

14. Pets a b c d

15. Grow Something 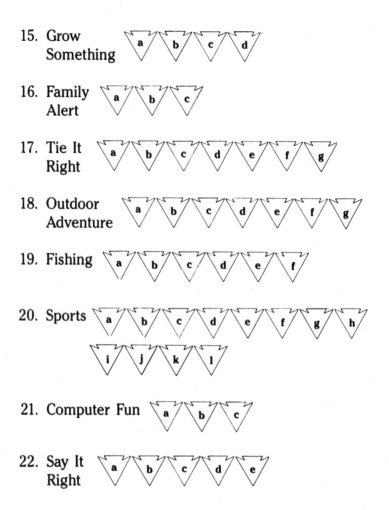 a b c d

16. Family Alert   a b c

17. Tie It Right   a b c d e f g

18. Outdoor Adventure   a b c d e f g

19. Fishing   a b c d e f

20. Sports   a b c d e f g h i j k l

21. Computer Fun   a b c

22. Say It Right   a b c d e